PREPARING MY HEART
for ADVENT

a Spiritual
Pilgrimage
for the
Christmas
Season

PREPARING MY HEART
for ADVENT

a Spiritual Pilgrimage for the Christmas Season

Ann Marie Stewart

Advancing the Ministries of the Gospel

AMG Publishers

God's Word to you is our highest calling.

Preparing My Heart for Advent:
A Spiritual Pilgrimage for the Christmas Season

Published by AMG Publishers. All Rights Reserved.

First Printing, 2005

ISBN: 0-89957-083-6

Map design by Sherrill Kraakmo/White Leaf Design, promotional photo by Jon and Amy Harris

Cover design by Daryle Beam and Craig Eller at Market Street Design, Chattanooga, TN

Interior design and typesetting by PerfecType, Nashville, TN

Editing by Candy Arrington and Rick Steele

Printed in the United States of America

10 09 08 07 06 05 –EB– 6 5 4 3 2 1

Dedicated to my Aunt Lydia Harris,
a writer, prayer warrior, encourager, and friend

Acknowledgments

My heart is prepared to thank my friends and family. Thank you Bill and Ruth Roetcisoender (Mom and Dad), and my two brothers Brad and Brian Roetcisoender for your continued support; Leesburg United Methodist Bible study groups who helped me "test-drive" the studies; Veronica Roetcisoender for technical assistance; and my sister-in-law Caroline Roetcisoender for being the source of great material.

For their faithful prayer support, I thank Lydia and Milt Harris, Glenn and Helen Garner, Carrie Leslie, Jill Dye, Holly G. Coe, Leslie Williams, Barbara Boughton, Kim Domin, Jodi Musgrove, Joan McClenny, Marci Andrews, Anne Miller, Barbara Curtis, Rachelle Knight, and Karen van der Riet.

And for generous editing assistance, thanks to Lydia Harris, Glenn and Helen Garner, Carrie Leslie, Marci Andrews, and Tina Fetterly.

And for *preparing my heart* to write this book, I must thank two friends I've never met: Beth Moore and Philip Yancey. Beth Moore's studies have blessed my life, especially *Jesus the One and Only* and *A Woman's Heart: God's Dwelling Place*. Philip Yancey's *The Jesus I Never Knew* helped me know Jesus anew and offered a whole new look at His birth.

I thank my new friends Dan Penwell and Rick Steele at AMG for believing in *preparing hearts for Advent* and for preparing me to write through encouragement, prayer, and instruction. Special thanks also to Candy Arrington for her skillful editorial help.

Many thanks to my husband Will and daughters Christine and Julia for their patience and support.

Most of all thank you Jesus, the One who lives in my heart, whose birth I celebrate and whose second coming I await. Thank You Lord for giving me the love of words and the privilege of sharing Your story.

Ann Stewart

About the Author

ANN MARIE STEWART graduated with honors from the University of Washington and also earned the top educational honor awarded by the school for female education majors. Ann later conducted graduate studies in film and television at the University of Michigan and taught English and music for a number of years at various grade levels ranging from preschool to college-level. Ann currently writes a bi-monthly column entitled "Ann's Lovin Ewe" and performs as a vocal soloist.

Ann has conducted ample research for *Preparing My Heart for Advent.* Her expertise in choral conducting has helped her incorporate music into each week's lesson, while her background in acting and writing drama has allowed her to write this study in an expressive, engaging style. Ann's ultimate purpose for the book is that it would promote the sharing of ideas for preparing our hearts to reach out and share the Christmas story.

Ann and her husband and two daughters run a small sheep farm in Paeonian Springs, Virginia.

Introduction

After Thanksgiving, I take a deep breath and fly into Christmas. I play my favorite Christmas carols, haul out boxes of decorations, and schedule our family traditions and events. I may *plan* to make Christ the center of Christmas, but when I wait until December to focus on celebrating His birthday, I become entangled in Christmas lights, holiday baking, and festive engagements, often wondering if I've experienced that illusive "true meaning" of Christmas.

This year on December 26th, I'd like to reflect back on a Christmas spent in the presence of Immanuel. I want the whole month of December to be different. I long to look at my holiday season with eyes that see the *Christ* in *Christ*mas.

But how can I revisit the familiar Christmas story and see it anew? How can I see Christ in the symbols decorating the shopping malls? What do the words of my favorite carols really mean, and why were they written? How can December be a time for celebration as well as reflection? Perhaps it can happen if my heart is prepared in *November.*

Preparing My Heart for Advent is a women's Bible study which can be done in a group or on your own during the month of November. The intensive study is followed by devotional readings for December through Epiphany, January 6th. Each day of the November study corresponds with a December devotional reading. For example, you will study Joseph on *November* 12th and return to Joseph with a devotional reading on *December* 12th. The December devotional emphasis will keep you in the Word during the busiest season of the year.

Each week pauses for a look at a song, symbol, and suggestion. A familiar carol will be focused upon and its spiritual significance examined. It is my hope that the familiar carols will not be relegated this year to background music in department stores, but instead become personal and significant reminders to stop, look, listen, and experience Immanuel, God with us, wherever we are.

In addition to the carol, a symbol will be explained to help holiday decorations take on new meaning. And finally, you'll read a suggestion to prepare your heart to reach out and share the Christmas story.

Recognizing that women come in all sizes: married, unmarried, widowed, with and without children, the tips are *one-size-fits-all.* Knowing that women are often the heart of the home—especially during the Christmas season, we need to be spiritually prepared to celebrate Advent. But this is not a holiday how-to guide; it's a study to help focus on the *heart* preparations for Christmas.

This November, join me in looking at Christmas anew. I challenge you to immerse yourself in the scriptures as you study *Preparing My Heart for Advent*. Then in December, revisit and refresh your learning through the devotional emphasis. It is my prayer that on January 6th when you read your last Advent devotional reading, you'll realize this Christmas season was unique. Through study, your heart will be prepared for the Christ of Christmas before you are stuck with only the holly of the holidays.

Through study, reflection and preparation in November, may your heart be filled with joyful anticipation, and may your December be one of pondering anew a birth unlike any other.

Contents

Preparing my Heart for Advent

The Setting and Characters

November 1 Waiting for Jesus—Over 400 Years of Advent

Perhaps the Bible is very familiar to you, or maybe it's a little dusty from sitting on a shelf. Either way, this is a wonderful season to open your heart to learn more of what the Bible says.

When you pick up your Bible, you see most of it is Old Testament; yet we often concentrate our reading in the New Testament. In this study, we'll use both Old and New Testaments. Although the story of Christmas is primarily documented in the New Testament, the Old Testament also has much to say about Jesus' arrival. Understanding Old Testament prophecy and stories of God's people prior to God's arrival on earth is extremely important.

Did you know there is a chasm between the Old and New Testament? Your Bible may include reference material between the Old and New, but you may not realize that four hundred years of waiting happened between the end of Malachi and the beginning of Matthew.

What was happening to the people on earth as they awaited God's timing? To help us more fully prepare for Advent, today we'll look at the period of time preceding the arrival of Christ. Let's get started!

During the four-century gap between the Old and New Testaments, God was silent. Why? Some of the reasons may be found in the last two books of the Old Testament. The prophet Malachi revealed that the people of God offered blemished sacrifices, failed to show respect and honor to God (Malachi

1:6–7), violated the covenant with Levi, turned away from God's decrees, and withheld tithes (Malachi 3:6–9). They broke commitments with God, married non-Israelites, and divorced (Malachi 2:10–17). God warned, "I will be quick to testify against sorcerers, adulterers and perjurers, against those who defraud laborers of their wages, who oppress the widows and the fatherless, and deprive aliens of justice, but do not fear me" (Malachi 3:5).

Zechariah 7:11–13 offers further insight. Read these verses and record your response to the questions below:

> *But they refused to pay attention; stubbornly they turned their backs and stopped up their ears. They made their hearts as hard as flint and would not listen to the law or to the words that the LORD Almighty had sent by his Spirit through the earlier prophets. So the LORD Almighty was very angry. 'When I called, they did not listen; so when they called, I would not listen,' says the LORD Almighty.*

> hat about our hearts? When have we refused to pay attention to God's Word, turned a stubborn shoulder and been hard hearted? In what areas do we need softening this season?

1. What four actions did the Jewish people take?

_____

_____

_____

_____

2. What one action did God take?

_____

_____

3. How hard were their hearts?

_____

_____

God was silent to a people who would no longer listen. They experienced a famine of hearing the words of the Lord (Amos 8:11b). During a time when the surrounding Gentile,

Roman, and Greek religions all espoused beliefs in multiple gods, the one true God was silent. The centuries between testaments were not kind to the Jewish faith.

After their exile in Babylonia, the Jews were ruled by Persia, then Greece. The Jewish faith and practices were stifled; reading of the law, circumcision, and observance of the Sabbath were all banned by Antiochus IV.[1] Much to the horror of the Jews, a statue of the Greek God Zeus was placed in the temple of Jerusalem, and pigs were sacrificed on the altar.[2] This led to the Maccabean revolt in 167 BC and the birth of the Jewish celebration of Hanukkah. The Jews wanted to keep the temple lanterns burning but had oil for only one night. They believed a miracle allowed the oil to burn for eight consecutive nights.[3]

Greek rule was followed by Roman rule. Although the reign of Caesar Augustus, part of the period known as the "Peace of Rome" or *Pax Romana* (27 BC to AD 180), was less violent, the Romans controlled all Europe, North Africa, and the shores of the Mediterranean. Whether under Roman or Greek rule, the Jews were oppressed, persecuted, and had to submit to the foreign constraint of their sacred customs. Still, they clung to their religious traditions and the ancient promise of a Messiah.

What is your hope? What are you longing for this Christmas?

In *The Bible Jesus Read*, Philip Yancey describes their dim hope,

> A general malaise set in among the Jews, a low-grade disappointment with God that showed in their complaints and also in their actions. As the people expressed it then, "It is futile to serve God. What did we gain by carrying out his requirements…?" That final question troubled the Jews for centuries after Malachi and the remaining prophets had faded from the scene. They saw no miracles, no spectacular interventions, and heard no new words from the Lord. Had God forgotten how to be merciful? Had he plugged his ears against their groans? The Old Testament ends on a note of disappointment, unfulfilled longings, and faint hope.[4]

The Old Testament ends with the book of Malachi and a people who wanted a King like David, a Good Shepherd, a Savior, and a sympathetic ruler who would represent them. *And the government will be upon his shoulders...* The Old Testament ends with that hope.

Though four hundred years separate the Old and the New, the last words of the Old Testament perfectly segue into the opening of the New Testament. Malachi 4:5–6 reads:

> *See, I will send you the prophet Elijah before that great and dreadful day of the LORD comes. He will turn the hearts of the fathers to their children, and the hearts of the children to their fathers; or else I will come and strike the land with a curse.*

"Elijah?" you ask. "Elijah from the Old Testament is returning?" No, but we have a *New Testament* Elijah. He first appears in Luke 1:13 when God breaks His silence by speaking to Zechariah, the New Testament Elijah's father. And who is this New Testament Elijah? He is none other than that eccentric, locust-eating prophet, John the Baptist.

Malachi reports the word of the Lord Almighty concerning John, "See, I will send my messenger, who will prepare the way before me. Then suddenly the Lord you are seeking will come to his temple; the messenger of the covenant, whom you desire, will come" (Malachi 3:1). John the Baptist is the messenger, the New Testament Elijah. And he is the one who would prepare the way for the Messiah.

In the first gospel of the New Testament, which was specifically written with Jewish readers in mind, Matthew relates exactly what Jews need to determine the lineage of their Messiah. The opening verse of the New Testament explains that Jesus is the Son (or descendent) of David and the Son of Abraham. Jesus is the One for whom the Jewish people have waited for millennia. Verse 17 of Matthew 1 explains that Jesus arrives in the perfection of the fullness of time: fourteen generations plus fourteen generations plus fourteen generations (see Matthew 1:17).

But when the time had fully come, God sent his Son, born of a woman, born under law, to redeem those under law, that we might receive the full rights of sons. (Galatians 4:4–5)

The time is right. Greek rule has left a common language; the Romans have created a communication system; this combined with the relative peacefulness in Rome will allow the gospel to be delivered.[5]

In the fullness of time, God delivers His Word. God speaks with Zechariah, Mary, Joseph, and the shepherds. God prepares them for His greatest reconnection: God in the flesh coming to earth. "But when the time had fully come, God sent his Son, born of a woman" (Galatians 4:4). And how does God choose to reveal Himself? Philip Yancey writes,

> Among people who walled off a separate sanctum for God in the temple and shrank from pronouncing or spelling out the name, God made a surprise appearance as a baby in a manger. What can be less scary than a newborn with his limbs wrapped tight against his body? In Jesus, God found a way of relating to human beings that did not involve fear.[6]

We rejoice over the reconnection and the new relationship we have through Christ's birth, and we celebrate the baby in the manger on Christmas Day. However, this study is not called "Preparing my Heart for *Christmas*" because this study is about preparing our hearts for much more than that. It's about *Advent*, a word unfamiliar to many.

The Latin word for "advent" means "the coming." The advent season was instituted as a time of fasting for holy living, and it remains a time of inward preparation for the commemoration of the coming of Christ. It's much more than a one-day celebration, it's a month to be still and remember the God of our past, present, and future. In anticipating His first coming, we celebrate His presence in the present, and prepare for His second coming to earth.

How can you experience Christmas anew this year?

Pause and Apply: Each day of November you are preparing your heart for Advent. You will be knee-deep in the Old Testament as well as the New. Consider with great anticipation the arrival of the baby who is God in flesh. The time is full for you to celebrate renewal with God and a rewarding relationship with His Son, Jesus.

November 2 Reflecting and Reporting

Today we'll read the Christmas story. Does it seem too early? Maybe it doesn't even feel necessary. After all, you already know the story. If it seems you've heard it again and again and again, perhaps you have!

Let's look at this passage as if we've never heard the story. Read it as if for the first time, and look for what isn't clear. Believe me, you'll have questions! As a matter of fact, I have been determined to write down all the questions I have about the Christmas story. And in my questioning, I seek to better understand what God wants me to learn from His Word.

📖 Read Luke 1 through 2:40, asking questions. Luke was the BC (Before Christ) and AD (After Christ's birth) reporter, but this week you're the 21st century investigator asking the *Who, What, When, Where, Why, and How* questions.

Write one question you have using each of the six *W*s and the one *H* listed below. Example:

Who were Luke's sources?

Why did Mary head for the hills to see Elizabeth?

What was Joseph thinking when Mary was at Elizabeth's?

Where, exactly, did the Magi come from?

When was Mary's mother told? Before or after Mary's visit with Elizabeth?

How did Mary's mother react to the news of her daughter's pregnancy?

Now it's your turn:

Who

_____

Why

_____

What

_____

Where

_____

When

_____

How

_____

Pause and Apply: Though it's fun to ask questions and speculate, we need to remember that the Holy Spirit guided the writers to record certain important and pertinent data. Therefore, what God has given us in His Word is enough. Our part is to try to understand it and apply it to our lives. As you dive into the Word each day, pray for the Holy Spirit to help you understand the scriptures and live by them daily.

November 3 The Characters in Our Story

In yesterday's reading, you were introduced to twelve major players. Let's learn about their roles in the story by examining their actions and character qualities.

Scan Luke 1—2:40. Look for the individuals listed below and note their significance and at least one character quality. Don't worry if you can't find all of the answers. You'll find additional information in tomorrow's reading of Matthew.

Name	Role	Character Qualities
Herod	King	suspicious, jealous
Gabriel		
Zechariah		
Elizabeth		
John the Baptist		
Mary		
Joseph		
Simeon		
Anna		
Jesus		
Shepherds		
Magi		

Pause and Apply: God used quite a cast of characters to complete the Christmas story. You are a part of that story.

What are your strong character qualities and strengths? List them below. How can you use them for the glory of God?

_____

_____

_____

_____

_____

_____

November 4 Another Look at the Christmas Story

Luke was a thorough reporter, his book being the longest in the New Testament. The other Gospels—Matthew, Mark, and John—each handle the Christmas story differently. Today we'll take a look at all the Gospels or the books of *good news*.

1. Read Matthew 1:18 through Chapter 2 and fill in any additional information you find about the twelve major players on yesterday's chart.

2. What information in the Matthew chapters is *not* a part of Luke 1—2:40, and 3:23–38?

_____

_____

3. What information in Luke chapters 1 and 2 and Luke 3:23–38 is *not* a part of Matthew chapters 1 and 2?

_____

_____

Many have undertaken to draw up an account of the things that have been fulfilled among us, just as they were handed down to us by those who from the first were eyewitnesses and servants of the word. Therefore, since I myself have carefully investigated everything from the beginning, it seemed good also to me to write an orderly account for you, most excellent Theophilus, so that you may know the certainty of the things you have been taught. (Luke 1:1–4)

Luke opens his writing with the explanation that "many have undertaken to draw up an account of the things that have been fulfilled among us" (Luke 1:1). And he follows by explaining that the sources are eyewitness accounts (verse 2). His description that things have been "fulfilled" reveals he understands Jesus as the fulfillment to Old Testament prophecy. Luke addresses his letter to Theophilus, which in Greek means "lover of God,"[7] "dear to God," or "friend of God."[8] Luke's educated, Greek speaking audience has already heard the story; now Luke wants them to know it with certainty.

4. Knowing that Matthew was a tax collector writing for the Jews, and Luke a doctor writing for the Gentiles, how does this correspond with their unique writing style and coverage?

_____

_____

_____

5. Looking at Luke 1:1–4, what do we know about the authenticity of Luke's writing?

_____

_____

_____

Not only does Luke claim accuracy, his account lists historical figures and events. Luke mentions Caesar Augustus and the registration in Bethlehem.

6. Glance over the first chapters of the other two Gospels of John and Mark. What is absent from their writings?

_____

_____

Matthew emphasizes Jesus as King. Luke emphasizes Jesus as the Son of Man. Mark was a missionary, who wrote about miracles and action. With Mark, everything seems to happen *immediately!* Mark wrote primarily to the Romans and Gentiles, showing Christ as a Servant, Savior, and Son of God. About forty percent of his book details Christ's last week on earth.[9]

Matthew, Mark, and Luke are called the Synoptic Gospels. In Greek *syn* means "with" and *optic* means "eye." It means that Matthew, Mark, and Luke are meant to be seen together.[10] John's gospel differs greatly.

John was a wealthy Jew who was later nicknamed by Jesus a *Son of Thunder* (see Mark 3:17), and he is widely recognized to be the *disciple whom Jesus loved* (see John 21:20, 24). John's writings emphasize that since the beginning, God and Jesus were One. Jesus has been in existence long before AD or BC. He's been here before all time.

7. Though John 1:9–14 never spells out the name Jesus, John uses other words to describe Him. Underline three of these descriptions from the passages below.

> IN THE *beginning was the Word, and the Word was with God, and the Word was God. He was with God in the beginning. Through him all things were made; without him nothing was made that has been made. In Him was life, and that life was the light of men. The light shines in the darkness, but the darkness has not understood it (John 1:1–5).*

> *The true light that gives light to every man was coming into the world. He was in the world, and though the world was made through him, the world did not recognize him. He came to that which was his own, but his own did not receive him. Yet to all who received him, to those who believed in his name, he gave the right to become children of God—children born not of natural descent, nor of human decision or a husband's will, but born of God. The Word became flesh and made his dwelling among us. We have seen his glory, the glory of the One and Only, who came from the Father, full of grace and truth (John 1:9–14).*

Indeed, Jesus is the Word, the Life, and the Light. These three words describe Jesus; but John goes on to say that Jesus describes God. Jesus is the earthly representation of His Father. John 1:18 says, "he hath declared him," (KJV), "He has interpreted Him, and He has made Him known" (AMPLIFIED), and my favorite, "He has explained Him" (NASB). What a wonderful description. Because of God's tender mercy, He came up with a plan to explain Himself through His Son.

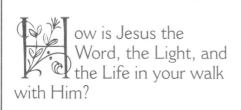

How is Jesus the Word, the Light, and the Life in your walk with Him?

Pause and Apply: Keep looking for ways to better understand God through the Word. In what ways do you hope to see God explained through Jesus this Christmas?

And how will your own actions explain the difference Christ has made in your life? The New Testament begins with four Gospel writers with different occupations and audiences sharing the good news with accuracy and enthusiasm. We, too, come with differing backgrounds and we meet a variety of audiences. How could your personal experiences, interests, and stories be useful in sharing the gospel this Christmas season?

> *No one has ever seen God, but God the One and Only, who is at the Father's side, has made him known.* (John 1:18)

November 5 A Busy First Christmas

We sometimes think our lives are hectic. Today we'll look at the order of events involving the birth of Jesus. By attempting to log the order, we'll gain perspective into the chronology. We'll divide the events into three sections: before Jesus' Birth, Bethlehem, and after Jesus' birth.

📖 Using Matthew 1:18 through the end of chapter 2, and Luke chapters 1 and 2,

1. Next to each event, write down one of the following chronological descriptions: **Before Jesus' Birth, Bethlehem,** or **After Jesus' Birth**.

2. Number the events in each column chronologically.

3. Place each of your event numbers on the timeline.

Sometimes the order and times between events are unclear, so work in pencil!

Events:

- Mary and Joseph discover Herod has died, so they return to Nazareth.
- Gabriel appears to Mary and tells her that she will be the mother of the Messiah.
- An angel appears to Joseph, warning him to flee to Egypt. Joseph obeys.
- Mary and Joseph become engaged.
- Mary is with child from the Holy Spirit
- Because they must register for the census, Mary and Joseph journey to Bethlehem.

- An angel appears to Zechariah and tells him Elizabeth will bear a son.
- The angel appears to the shepherds with good news. They hasten to find their King.
- Eight days after his birth, Jesus is circumcised.
- An angel appears to Joseph in a dream telling him to take Mary as his wife.
- Mary gives birth to her firstborn son.
- Mary leaves in haste for Aunt Elizabeth's home in Judea.
- Obeying the angel, Joseph takes Mary as his wife.
- Mary and Joseph go to Jerusalem to present Jesus to His Father.
- Herod kills all of Bethlehem's boys under the age of two.
- Elizabeth goes into seclusion for five months.
- Joseph plans to dismiss Mary quietly.
- Joseph is warned in a dream and takes Mary and Jesus to Nazareth.

Event Timeline

4. Star the events that seem difficult to place on the timeline.

5. Number the Magi events below and then add them to the timeline below:

- Herod calls for the Magi.
- The Magi have a bad dream and do not return to Herod.
- Studying scripture and the stars, the Magi decide to seek out the King of the Jews.
- The Magi come to Jerusalem.
- Herod hears of the Magi and inquires of *others* where Jesus will be born.
- The star stops over the child.
- The Magi kneel down and worship the baby Jesus.

Event Timeline

6. Using the map and the listed routes below, draw arrows to show the travels of Mary and Joseph.

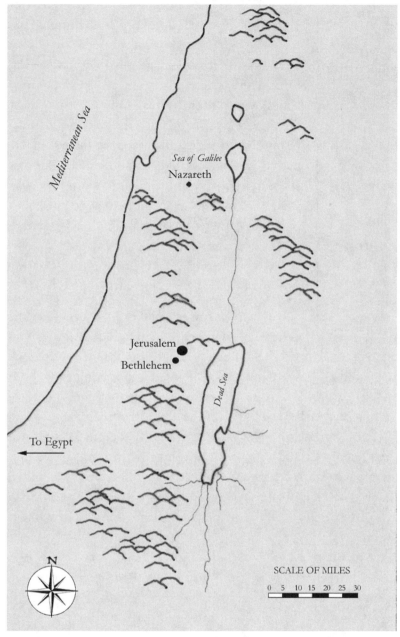

- ❏ Mary travels to Judea
- ❏ Mary and Joseph journey to Bethlehem
- ❏ Mary and Joseph take Jesus to Jerusalem then back to Bethlehem.
- ❏ Joseph, Mary, and Jesus flee to Egypt.
- ❏ Joseph takes Jesus and Mary to Nazareth.

Pause and Apply: Mary's timeline was complicated, but it was all in God's time. What about your timeline? It may seem too early to consider your December calendar, but how will you keep it uncluttered?

In November, my cousin Joan sits down with her family of six and highlights days on December's calendar. These are special family times, and nothing can crowd out these evenings. Other people list the activities that are important to them, making sure the events are placed on the December calendar. Save time and space to keep an unhurried peace. You may even need to schedule in a "snow day" or a day of play. Plan now to make certain your December schedule reflects your true priorities.

November 6 The Genealogy of Christ

Matthew 1 and Luke 3:23–38 include the genealogy of Christ. In previous readings you may have skipped the tedious lists because of boredom or lack of familiarity with unfamiliar names, wondering why both Matthew and Luke devoted so many verses to genealogies.

Today we'll focus on a few of the individuals God placed in Christ's lineage. The next few days are perhaps the most challenging of all, but possibly the most intriguing. Be prepared for surprises! We'll look at a few *characters* (literally!) each day. Hang in there, and be prepared to use the index in the front of your Bible to help you find the Old Testament books.

Read Matthew 1:1–17 and Luke 3:23–38.

The genealogy is given twice. At first glance the two genealogies may seem very similar; however, we note a few differences.

1. Where does Matthew's begin and end?

_____

Where does Luke's begin and end?

_____

> What steps can you take to plan for a gentle Christmas?
>
> What do you look forward to doing this Christmas?

2. Besides being in reverse order, which section of names is missing in Matthew's list?

_____

_____

The lineages are the same from Abraham to David, but after that they differ. There are many thoughts on this. Some surmise one is the natural or bloodline and the other is the legal line. Others speculate Luke's genealogy is Mary's, and Matthew's genealogy is Joseph's. Note the difference in Matthew 1:16 and Luke 3:23. Joseph's father is Jacob (1:16), yet Joseph's father by marriage (father-in-law) appears to be Eli (verse 3:23).[11]

3. Why do you think Joseph's line is revealed?

_____

_____

_____

4. Another difference is that Matthew's genealogy lists five women. Write their names below.

_____

_____

_____

Are these names familiar to you? We'll come back to study the significance of these five women in a later lesson.

Abraham/Isaac

📖 Read Genesis 21:1–20, and chapter 22 (especially verses 17–18).

The Messiah had to be a son of Abraham and a son of David. In a few days we'll look at David, but today let's focus on Abraham and his son, Isaac.

5. Why are Abraham and Isaac significant? What relationship does theirs foreshadow?

_____

_____

_____

God promised Abraham that his descendants would be as numerous as the stars in the sky, and yet God also asked Abraham to sacrifice his son, Isaac (Genesis 22:1–18). It seems contradictory, yet Abraham trusted God and said, "God himself will provide the lamb for the burnt offering, my son." At the altar, after an angel intervenes, Abraham "looked up and there in a thicket he saw a ram caught by its horns. He went over and took the ram and sacrificed it as a burnt offering instead of his son" (verse 13).

According to both the Old and New Testaments, Abraham's words are prophetic. In this Old Testament passage, Isaac was supposed to be the sacrifice, but God provided a ram as the substitute. In the New Testament, God provided a lamb for all of us. He provided *His* only Son Jesus Christ.

6. In Genesis 22:17–18, what four promises does God give Abraham? Place a check by any you know have been fulfilled.

_____

_____

_____

_____

_____

_____

> *"Look up at the heavens and count the stars—if indeed you can count them. . . . So shall your offspring be."* (Genesis 15:5)
>
> *"I will establish my covenant as an everlasting covenant between me and you and your descendants after you for the generations to come, to be your God and the God of your descendants after you."* (Genesis 17:7)

Pause and Apply: God keeps His promises. Have you studied the promises of God? If so, do you claim them in your own life? You can purchase a book of them or you can dig into the Word and research them. Find one today to stick on your bathroom mirror. Claim it for this month!

November 7 Song, Symbol, and Suggestion:
A Carol to Remember

About eight hundred years after Jesus was born, an unknown monk, schooled in prophecy, wrote a scripture-filled carol, linking the Old and New Testaments. "O Come, O Come, Emmanuel" taught many aspects of the Messiah during a time when average people had little access to the Bible. The words were coupled with a fifteenth-century Franciscan processional entitled "Veni Emmanuel." After missionary John Neale discovered and then translated the Latin chant into English in 1851, this hauntingly beautiful carol became popular.

Song: "O Come, O Come Emmanuel"

O come, O come Emmanuel,
And ransom captive Israel
That mourns in lonely exile here
Until the Son of God appear

CHORUS
Rejoice! Rejoice! Emmanuel
Shall come to thee, O Israel.
(Isaiah 7:14)

O come thou rod of Jesse, free
Thine own from Satan's tyranny
From depths of hell thy people save
And give them vict'ry o'er the grave
(Isaiah 11:1–10)

CHORUS
O come, Thou Dayspring, come and cheer
Our spirits by thine advent here
And drive away the shades of night
And pierce the clouds and bring us light
(Malachi 4:2)

CHORUS
O come, Thou Key of David, come
And open wide our heavenly home
Make safe the way that leads on high
And close the path to misery
(Isaiah 22:22)

CHORUS

With what you've learned about the chasm between the Old and New Testaments, you can hear how the song reflects the Jews' desire for a king like David. This chant, set in a minor key with much stepwise motion, and often sung *a cappella,* sounds melancholy in its longing. Rich with Old Testament scripture, this carol

> *Therefore the Lord himself will give you a sign: The virgin will be with child and will give birth to a son, and will call him Immanuel. (Isaiah 7:14)*
>
> *The virgin will be with child and will give birth to a son, and they will call him Immanuel"—which means, "God with us." (Matthew 1:23)*

> *But for you who revere my name, the sun of righteousness will rise with healing in its wings. And you will go out and leap like calves released from the stall. (Malachi 4:2)*

> *I will place on his shoulder the key to the house of David; what he opens no one can shut, and what he shuts no one can open. (Isaiah 22:22)*

will prepare you for next week's study of Old Testament prophecy fulfilled.

Our promised Messiah has come. He is Emmanuel, Rod of Jesse, Dayspring, Key of David. Now we, too, can rejoice! Rejoice! Emmanuel has come!

Symbol: Christmas Tree[12]

I love it when our newly cut Christmas tree is decorated. The fragrance of evergreen branches fills the air, and lights twinkle in the darkened living room, kindling memories from Christmases past. But the Christmas tree is not merely eye candy; it can be a reminder of God's love—evergreen and everlasting.

Although having a tree in the home began a thousand years after the birth of Christ and is probably rooted in pagan culture, its meaning has changed over the years. The tradition may have begun with the Nordic people who superstitiously brought evergreen trees in their homes during the dark of winter to bring in the gift of strength. Other cultures and groups continued using the symbolism of the mysterious evergreen in their worship.

But in the 7th century, a sacred spin was added when a monk named St. Boniface used the evergreen to teach that the everlasting nature of the evergreen reminds us of the eternal life we can have in Christ, and the tree's triangular outline can represent Father, Son, and Holy Spirit.

Some say the first Christmas tree appeared in Strasbourg, Alsace (a region of France) in 1605. Another story connects Martin Luther with the first lighted Christmas tree. This legend says Martin Luther was so captivated by starlight reflecting on evergreens that he came home and tied candles to the boughs of a tree inside his home. Luther taught that the tree's colors are evergreen, just as God's love is evergreen, and the candles remind us of the hope Jesus Christ brought into a dark world.

Now when you smell the greenery, remember that God's love is everlasting and evergreen. The shape of the tree points heavenward—point your heart there as well. Let the twinkling lights remind you that Jesus is your hope and light in a dark world. As you gaze at the star atop the tree, think about the Magi's pursuit of the King, and remember to follow Jesus all year round. The angel decoration can remind you of the good news you have to share with others.

God gave you many senses to experience the pleasure of a Christmas tree. Thank Him for all these senses, and use them to remind you of God's everlasting love and light.

Suggestion: Give the Gift of a Christmas Tree

I'm always saddened when I hear about someone wearied by the burden of Christmas, saying "I decided not to put up a tree this year. It's too much work." Although the celebration of Christmas doesn't necessitate a Christmas tree, for an elderly person or shut-in who can't decorate a tree, but who would still enjoy the fragrance and lights, maybe you can provide an alternative.

Find that special someone who might not be planning to decorate a Christmas tree this year. Purchase a small, real, or artificial tree. Then involve others in decorating it. The ideas below will get you started.

1. Ask neighbors to donate one extra ornament from their own trees.

2. Make homemade ornaments out of pictures of neighbors. Ask for a school picture or snapshot from everyone on your street. If there are children in the neighborhood, have them cut a circle around their pictures and paste them on colored paper. The kids can further decorate their ornament with glitter glue.

3. Skip the ornaments and buy a large roll of red and gold ribbon and tie bows all over the tree! Share the significance of the Christmas colors: green for God's everlasting love, red for Jesus' death on the cross, and gold for eternal life.

4. Perhaps you could ask ten women in your Bible study group to write down their favorite verses on a red or green circle and let the real meaning of Christmas be read through the ornaments on the tree. Call them "trimmings in truth"!

5. Remember, it doesn't have to be a *real 3-D* tree! Cut out a tag board tree and collect faces of those in your friend's neighborhood. Glue the homemade picture ornaments to the tree and outline each ornament in glitter glue.

6. Try a "helping hand" tree. Cut out a tag board tree and trace the hands of all your neighbors. Glue them to the tree as

evergreen branches. For an added gift, have the owners of these "helping hands" write something they could do for the recipient over the course of the next year.

7. For another spiritual alternative, consider a tree filled with symbols of the names for Christ. One friend of mine and her kindergartener made all their own ornaments: a crown for King of Kings, a snowflake signifying Christ's washing us whiter than snow, and a small goblet representing the Last Supper and the New Covenant.

Similarly, the Chrismon tree is decorated with monogram ornaments of Christ bedecked in white and gold depicting Christ's holiness and royalty.

8. Family Life Today publishes a box of ornaments depicting the names of Christ entitled "Adornaments."[13] My children love to go through the collection of ornaments and call out each name for Christ.

Names of Christ
Immanuel: Matthew 1:23
The Door: John 10:9
The True Vine: John 15:5
The Giver of Living Water: John 4:10
The Light of the World: John 8:12
The Bright Morning Star: Revelation 22:16
The Lion from the Tribe of Judah: Revelation 5:5
The Lamb of God: John 1:29
The Good Shepherd: John 10:11
The King of Kings and Lord of Lords: 1 Timothy 6:15
The Bread of Life: John 6:35
The Savior: 1 John 4:14–15

Can you imagine the joy a neighborhood tree could bring to a lonely person? I can almost hear the grateful recipient brag, "Have you seen *my* tree this year?"

No matter what tree or decorations you select, be prepared to share what the Christmas tree stands for and make a date to return for an "undecorating" party. The promise of your presence for an extra visit will not only relieve your friend of a burden, but also be something special he or she can look forward to after the holidays.

What is something the Lord has placed on your heart to try this Christmas?

WEEK TWO

The Old and the New

November 8 Surprises in the Lineage

The two New Testament genealogies introduced last week are filled with Old Testament characters. Who are those characters and why did God list them? Let's find out by digging a little deeper into these genealogies. Remember your list of five women? Today we'll study two of them: Rahab and Tamar, beginning with Tamar, who conceived a son named Perez with her father-in-law Judah (see Genesis 38:6–30; 1 Chronicles 2:4).

After Tamar's husband dies, Judah ignores the customs of the time and wrongfully withholds his youngest son from becoming Tamar's husband and father of future children. So, Tamar disguises herself as a harlot, and while disguised, has sexual relations with Judah. When Judah hears of his daughter-in-law's pregnancy, he is appalled until she reveals he shared in the sex act and is the baby's father. Talk about the plot to a bad soap opera! Yet Judah and Tamar, as well as their son, are recorded in Matthew's genealogy of Jesus.

I have to wonder why. Could it be that God included these individuals to help us understand that His purposes are realized through less than perfect people?

📖 We have not one, but two prostitutes in the lineage. Read Joshua 2:1–24 to learn about a woman who, despite her occupation, put her trust in God rather than men.

When Joshua and his company of spies search Jericho, Rahab hides them. Her reason? She recognizes all that God has accomplished for the Israelites.

1. What does Rahab say to the men at the end of verse 11? *For the LORD your God is. . . .*

_____

Rahab lets the spies down by a rope through the window. As they leave, they advise her to tie a cord of scarlet thread in the window to distinguish her home and keep it safe during the coming assault. Rahab and her family are spared when the spies and army return to conquer the inhabitants of Jericho.

> an you claim, "For the LORD is *my* God in heaven above and on the earth below?"

It's interesting to compare this scarlet cord with the blood of the lamb marking the Israelites' doors during the Plague. The bloodstain preserved the firstborn in each family. The death angel literally "passed over." This "passing over" marked the beginning of the celebration of Passover (Exodus 11:5–6; 12:3–7, 11–14).

Similarly, the mark of Christ's blood, which we remember on Good Friday, preserves every believer. Christmas can hardly be celebrated without thinking beyond Jesus' birth to the sacrifice, death, and resurrection of Good Friday and Easter. God allowed His only Son, an innocent lamb, to die that we might be saved.

📖 Now fast-forward four chapters to Joshua 6:1–27.

We are not given full details about the rest of Rahab's life. She must have chosen to follow God and marry into the Jewish faith, for later she bears a son included in the lineage of Christ. Hebrews 11:31 confirms and affirms that by faith Rahab the Harlot did not perish.

Pause and Apply: How does the inclusion of Judah, Tamar, and Rahab make you feel about your own personal mistakes and successes? If someone felt unworthy of coming to Christ, what could you say to encourage him or her?

If you have time and want to look at a few more people in the genealogy, the Old Testament includes a variety of good and bad kings (unfortunately, far more bad than good). In many cases, the ungodly kings led God's people into perverse lifestyles and idol worship. The consequences were severe. Centuries earlier, when Samuel ruled as the last of the Judges, he predicted that God's chosen race would turn from the Lord. Samuel's warnings were unheeded by the multitudes who longed for a king. In Samuel's day, the people of Israel wanted to be like the surrounding nations and empires that were ruled by absolute monarchs, and the people got their way—against Samuel's better judgment. Just as Israel emulated the surrounding nations in its choice of government, its people eventually went chasing after those nations' pagan gods and wanton lifestyles. At one point, the nation split into two nations, Israel in the north and Judah in the south. None of the Kings of Israel "did right in the sight of the Lord" during this time, while a few good kings were sprinkled among many bad ones in the nation of Judah. Several kings out of the nation of Judah (good and bad) appear in the messianic genealogy lists found in Matthew 1:1–17 and Luke 3:23–38. Two kings we will examine today are Manasseh and his grandson Josiah. Read the Scripture passages below relating to each of these kings.

Manasseh	**Josiah**
2 Chronicles 33:1–20	2 Chronicles 34:1–7, (esp. verses 2 and 31–33)
2 Kings 21:1–18	2 Kings 22:1–7, (esp. verses 2 and 18–20)

Manasseh was a notorious king who did evil in the sight of the Lord. He rebuilt the high places for idol worship his father Hezekiah had broken down, erected altars for the Baals, worshiped and served all the hosts of heaven, practiced witchcraft and sorcery, used divination, visited mediums and spiritists, and shed innocent blood. Need I say more? The Bible says he provoked God to anger. I can see why!

In contrast, his grandson Josiah "did what was right in the eyes of the LORD and walked in the ways of his father David, not turning aside to the right or to the left" (2 Chronicles 34:2). Josiah's heart was tender; he humbled himself before the Lord and was obedient. Josiah removed the abominations from all the lands belonging to the sons of Israel, instructed all who were present in Israel to serve the Lord, tore down the altars, and repaired the house of God. King Josiah made a covenant before the Lord to walk after Him, keep His commandments, testimonies, and statutes with all his heart and soul. During his lifetime, the Israelites did not turn from following the Lord God.

We examine the lives of Manasseh and Josiah today to point out that even the messianic bloodline is sprinkled with those who are better candidates for the hall of shame rather than the hall of fame. But God ultimately worked His perfect will through the gene pool of some very flawed individuals. Isn't it neat how God works?

Pause and Apply: Perhaps your family line does not include a long list of believers. How does this story offer encouragement or challenge you to leave a positive family legacy?

November 9 A Woman Who Followed God: Ruth

Tucked into Matthew 1:5 is Ruth, wife of Boaz and the mother of Obed, and the third woman listed in Jesus' genealogy. An entire Old Testament book is devoted to her.

The book of Ruth foreshadows God's redemptive plan and illustrates God's sovereignty as He meets needs in both big and small ways. Ruth is one of the most beautiful stories in the Old Testament, not to mention that it's a pleasant and easy-to-read love story.

Before you begin, I'll give you some background on marriage and widowhood 1100 years before the Christmas story.

As we saw in the story of Tamar and Judah, if a woman became a widow, it was the responsibility of the husband's brother to marry the widow and carry on his deceased brother's name. If the deceased had no living brother, the law stated the responsibility went to the next of kin (see Deuteronomy 25:5, 7–10).

The next of kin would bear children in the deceased's name and bequeath a portion of his estate and property to these children. The responsibility could be rejected, but even the act of refusal had an appropriate procedure (with a sandal, no less)! With this background, read through the book of Ruth without stopping and enjoy the romance and courtship of Ruth and Boaz.

Read Ruth 1–4.

Due to economic and agricultural famine, Naomi and her husband Elimelech leave Bethlehem to sojourn to a distant land where he experiences spiritual famine. The word *"sojourned"* would indicate a temporary visit. However, Naomi and Elimelech remain; their sons marry outside of the faith; and linger another ten years. After Elimelech and Naomi's two sons die, Naomi is now poor both spiritually and economically. She leaves Moab to return to Bethlehem, the land of her people and faith. Ruth decides to follow her.

1. Whom did Ruth *know* she wanted to follow? (1:16)

_____

2. What would it take for Ruth to give up her homeland, religion, and her own family of origin for an unfamiliar region and religion?

_____

_____

_____

3. What character qualities in Boaz must have been attractive to Ruth?

_____

_____

_____

Boaz, who *just happens* to be from the same family as Naomi's husband, *just happens* to own the field where Ruth *just happens* to choose to glean. He *just happens* to possess the "finest of qualities." Boaz *just happens* to be a wealthy gentleman. Did all this *just happen* or could it be that God was at work in the lives of Boaz, Naomi, and Ruth for the ultimate good of His Kingdom? In God's world, there are no coincidences.

I want to laugh when I think how Boaz must have reacted when he awakened to a kind and beautiful servant at his feet. We see he became a man of action. Boaz knew how to handle the next steps to make Ruth his wife—by reacting promptly. Naomi says, "For the man will not rest until the matter is settled today" (3:18).

4. What character qualities in *Ruth* were attractive to *Boaz*?

In other words, why does he call her a "woman of excellence"? (3:11).

_____

_____

_____

We've been reading about lineages. Check out the lineage in Ruth 4:18–22. It begins with Perez. Remember Perez? He was the result of Judah and Tamar's incestuous relationship. Verses 21 and 22 record, "And to Salmon was born Boaz and to Boaz, Obed, and to Obed was born Jesse and to Jesse, David." The lineage lists Salmon as Boaz's *father*. But do you remember Boaz's *mother's* name? Flipping back to Matthew 1:5 you'll find that Boaz's mother was the prostitute Rahab! Boaz does not have a perfect background, and Boaz's own mother began outside the faith.

The lineage of Christ is a patchwork of famous and infamous characters. Some in this line entered this planet as a result of an adulterous or even incestuous relationship. King Solomon is a perfect example of one born out of adultery, and we will look at his story in tomorrow's study.

The messianic line is also a montage of various backgrounds and religions. The Book of Ruth reminds us that God welcomes all who believe in Him no matter their background or faith. He not only came for all, but His bloodline demonstrates His salvation for all.[14]

Now consider Naomi. In Ruth 1:11–13 we see her leaving Moab without any hope, telling her daughters they need not follow for there are no more sons in her womb.

> *Even if I thought there was still hope for me—even if I had a husband tonight and then gave birth to sons— would you wait until they grew up? Would you remain unmarried for them? No, my daughters. It is more bitter for me than for you, because the LORD's hand has gone out against me!" (Ruth 1:12–13).*

When she arrives in Bethlehem, she is almost unrecognizable to her old friends. Naomi, whose name means "pleasant," renames herself *Mara* meaning "bitter."

Don't call me Naomi," she told them. "Call me Mara, because the Almighty has made my life very bitter. I went away full, but the LORD has brought me back empty. Why call me Naomi? The LORD has afflicted me; the Almighty has brought misfortune upon me. (Ruth 1:20–21)

Despite Naomi's mourning, Ruth is a woman of faith and action. The most familiar verse in Ruth is 1:16: "Where you go I will go, and where you stay I will stay. Your people will be my people and your God my God."

Ruth is a foreigner, a Moabitess, and would not have been well received in Bethlehem. However, Ruth is quickly recognized as a woman of excellence. Why? She is a dedicated and resourceful servant whose love for her mother-in-law displays itself sacrificially and generously.

Ruth is an example to me. I wonder how many times my quiet service could—and should—reveal a deep, life-changing faith and commitment?

Boaz, too, is a positive example. I have two daughters. My prayer is that each will find a husband who is protective, caring, gentle, and kind. I hope my future sons-in-law will see spiritual beauty and be attracted to kindness, obedience, resourcefulness, and gentleness, and be men who could say, "May the LORD repay you for what you have done. May you be richly rewarded by the LORD, the God of Israel, under whose wings you have come to take refuge" (Ruth 2:12).

We read of the term *kinsman redeemer* in Isaiah 59:20. "The Redeemer will come to Zion, to those in Jacob who repent of their sins," declares the LORD. By definition, a kinsman redeemer must be related by blood and must pay a price.

5. How did Boaz redeem Ruth?

_____

_____

_____

6. How is Boaz, like Christ, a Kinsman Redeemer?

_____

_____

_____

Boaz is a Kinsman Redeemer preceding Christ our Redeemer. The women of Bethlehem say to Naomi, "Praise be to the LORD, who this day has not left you without a kinsman-redeemer. May he become famous throughout Israel!" (Ruth 4:14). They couldn't possibly know just how famous Boaz and his descendants would eventually be.

Of course the messianic line does not come through the unwilling and unnamed non-redeemer, and not even Mahlon, Ruth's first husband. It comes through Boaz, the kinsman-redeemer. Through Boaz and Ruth, King David will be born and ultimately our Redeemer, Jesus Christ.

November 10 A Man after God's Own Heart: David

Fast-forward three generations. Ruth and Boaz's son Obed has a son named Jesse who has a son named David. The David of *city of David*. The David as in *son of David*. The David as in *throne of David*. What's so special about *David*, anyway? Let's look at David's life and find out. I've summarized the scriptures below.

David's Heart: 1 Samuel 16:1–13.

Earlier we discussed Samuel and his unheeded advice regarding Israel selecting a king. Shortly afterward Saul becomes the nation's first king. After Saul's disappointing reign, the Lord "sought out a man after his own heart" (1 Samuel 13:14). When Samuel searches for the new king, God advises him,

"Do not consider his appearance or his height, for I have rejected him. The LORD does not look at the things man looks at. Man looks at the outward appearance, but the LORD looks at the heart" (1 Samuel 16:7).

God likes what he sees in the heart of a shepherd boy. At David's anointing, the Spirit of the Lord comes mightily upon him, preparing David for his new role.

David's Faith: 1 Samuel 17

Consider this scene: the Philistines are literally on one mountainside, the Israelites on another, with a valley between. The stakes are high: if one Israelite fights Goliath and wins, the

Philistines will become the Israelites' servants. But no Israelite is willing to take on the giant Goliath because a loss means the Israelites become servants of the Philistines.

Enter delivery boy David, bringing *in* some roasted grain, bread, and cheese, and hopefully, bringing *out* news from the front. Instead, David becomes the front line. He learns of Goliath's challenge and the potential rewards: great riches, the king's daughter in marriage, and freedom from work and taxes. After hearing Goliath taunt the armies of the living God, young David declares he'll fight the nearly ten-foot giant.

When others caution David because of his youth, he proclaims, "The LORD who delivered me from the paw of the lion and the paw of the bear, will deliver me from the hand of this Philistine" (1 Samuel 17:37). David refuses the traditional helmet and heavy armor, instead bearing his familiar five smooth stones and sling shot.

Goliath is insulted when David advances. "Am I a dog, that you come at me with sticks?" (verse 43). David answers with confidence because he knows the source of his strength, "You come against me with sword and spear and javelin, but I come against you in the name of the LORD Almighty, the God of the armies of Israel, whom you have defied" (verse 45). David recognizes the battle is the Lord's. Indeed, it takes but one of David's smooth stones, hitting precisely on Goliath's forehead, to bring victory to the Israelites.

David's Promise from God: 2 Samuel 7:4–17

David eventually becomes king over all of Israel. He continues to love God and increasingly wants to assume responsibilities for building the Lord's house. Read 2 Samuel 7:4–17 and note the many promises God makes to his chosen shepherd king.

1. (verse 9) _____
2. (verse 10) _____
3. (verse 11) _____
4. (verse 11) _____
5. (verse 12) _____

David's Praise: 2 Samuel 7:18–29

Though the Lord reveals that the privilege of building God's house will go to David's son, David responds with humility and praise,

> *For you know your servant, O Sovereign LORD. For the sake of your word and according to your will, you have done this great thing and made it known to your servant. How great you are, O Sovereign LORD! There is no one like you, and there is no God but you, as we have heard with our own ears (2 Samuel 7:20–22).*

Pause and Apply: David's praise often expressed itself through dancing and music as well as prayer. His praise must have been so pleasing to the Lord. How do we communicate with God? Could we strive for a relationship filled with praise?

David is recognized as a man after God's own heart. But David must have also understood that God searched David's own heart, for he instructs his son Solomon, the son chosen to build the temple, to "acknowledge the God of your father, and serve him with wholehearted devotion and with a willing mind, for the LORD searches every heart and understands every motive behind the thoughts" (1 Chronicles 28:9).

David's Temptation: 2 Samuel 11, 12:1–25

I'd like to say David's story of success was also a story of perfection. But just as none of us are perfect, neither was David. We mentioned in yesterday's study that David committed adultery with Bathsheba, and Solomon was a byproduct of that affair. (He was actually the second son born to David and Bathsheba, as the firstborn died in infancy.) But that's not all there is to this story, for David also had Bathsheba's husband killed before taking Bathsheba as his own wife. Most of us know the details of this sordid story. While on a rooftop, David's eyes land on a bathing beauty named Bathsheba, wife of Uriah the Hittite. David sends for Bathsheba to come into his chamber, and then he proceeds to have sex with her. When Bathsheba becomes pregnant, David orders her husband Uriah killed but makes it look like an unfortunate casualty of war. David then makes Bathsheba his wife.

It appears that David has covered his tracks so well that no one would ever discover what he had done. But of course he could not deceive God, and God has his ways of bringing things out in the open. To his credit, David eventually confesses his sin and asks God to forgive him (see 2 Samuel 12), but his life and kingdom begin to unravel in many areas. David's sins of adultery and murder, followed by his emotionally-distant style of parenting lead to family feuds, grossly flawed relationships with his children, and a dysfunctional family.

Though David's sin harvests dreadful consequences, God forgives him, and allows him to remain king for many years after. In spite of David's transgressions, God restores David to fellowship with him. Today David is regarded as Israel's greatest king, and his importance to the messianic bloodline is unparalleled. It is interesting to note that though Bathsheba did become David's wife and bore a son in the lineage of Christ (Solomon), she is still listed as "Uriah's wife" in Christ's genealogy in Matthew (1:6). God never wavers in His resolve to keep the marriage bed undefiled.

> When God searches your heart, what does He find? Worry less about what things look like on the outside, and prepare your heart for devotion to God. Pray today for pure motives and a loving heart.

David the Shepherd King: A Shepherd's Reflection: Psalm 23

David was a shepherd who knew what it meant to lay down his life for his sheep.

Look at 2 Samuel 5:2 and fill in the blank: "And the LORD said to you, 'You will _____ my people Israel, and you will become their _____.'"

Because of his background, he could pen, "The Lord is my shepherd." David had walked the valley of the shadow of death with impending evil surrounding him. David knew failure; David knew success. David was a man whose heart *turned to,* and later *returned to* God. David's life was measured from the inside out because his heart was after God's heart. David loved God, and God knew it.

Pause and Apply: What about us? Do we passionately love our Shepherd King who was born to lay down His life for us? We too can be like David with a heart filled with faith, praise, repentance, and trust.

Spend a few minutes with a psalm. Praise God in song or in prayer, and thank Him that He's your shepherd.

November 11 Old Testament Prophecy

I love the Old Testament, in part, because it adds background and depth to the teachings of the New Testament, but also because of its fascinating complexity and challenge. Though many of the scriptures were written for the Old Testament people, it is filled with prophecies regarding the New Testament, the Church Age, and apocalyptic events. Many messianic prophecies are found in Old Testament scripture. For example, Isaiah 7:14 states, "Therefore the Lord Himself will give you a sign: The virgin will be with child and will give birth to a son, and will call him Immanuel" (Isaiah 7:14).

This proclamation was delivered to King Ahaz. It had a dual prophetic purpose, for this king would have a son who would become King Hezekiah. However, the Immanuel prophecy also refers to the coming of our Messiah and is re-quoted in the New Testament passage of Matthew 1:18–25 to reveal the fulfillment of that prophecy.

All through the Old Testament, God foretells a coming Savior's arrival to earth. Discover in these treasures that God and Son were always One, and see how Jesus fulfills Old Testament prophecy.

1. Read the Old Testament scriptures below and <u>underline the portion</u> that reveals information about the coming Messiah.

Old Testament References to the Coming of the Messiah

"The days are coming," declares the LORD, "when I will raise up to David a righteous Branch, a King who will reign wisely and do what is just and right in the land" (Jeremiah 23:5).

In that day the branch of the LORD will be beautiful and glorious, and the fruit of the land will be the pride and glory of the survivors in Israel (Isaiah 4:2).

Listen, O high priest Joshua and your associates seated before you, who are men symbolic of things to come: I am going to bring my servant, the Branch (Zechariah 3:8).

"Tell him this is what the LORD Almighty says: 'Here is the man whose name is the Branch, and he will branch out from his place and build the temple of the LORD'" (Zechariah 6:12).

In those days and at that time I will make a righteous Branch sprout from David's line; he will do what is just and right in the land (Jeremiah 33:15).

A shoot will come up from the stump of Jesse; from his roots a Branch will bear fruit. The Spirit of the LORD will rest on him—the Spirit of wisdom and of understanding, the Spirit of counsel and of power, the Spirit of knowledge and of the fear of the LORD —and he will delight in the fear of the LORD. He will not judge by what he sees with his eyes, or decide by what he hears with his ears; but with righteousness he will judge the needy, with justice he will give decisions for the poor of the earth. He will strike the earth with the rod of his mouth; with the breath of his lips he will slay the wicked. Righteousness will be his belt and faithfulness the sash around his waist (Isaiah 11:1–5).

I see him, but not now; I behold him, but not near. A star will come out of Jacob, and a scepter will rise out of Israel (Numbers 24:17).

But you, Bethlehem Ephrathah, though you are small among the clans of Judah, out of you will come for me one who will be ruler over Israel, whose origins are from of old, from ancient times (Micah 5:2).

Not only is Jesus' birthplace prophesied, the Old Testament also describes Jesus' despised hometown (Isaiah 53:3; Psalm 22:6; with later confirmation in Matthew 2:23). Scripture states He would be a man of lowly and contemptible background, and we learn from New Testament accounts that Nazareth was not exactly the first place people thought of when thinking of the birthplace of royalty (see John 1:46). Nazareth may be related to the Hebrew word for "branch" (*neser* or *netser*) found in Isaiah 11:1, Jeremiah 23:5, Zechariah 3:8 and 6:12.[15] And so from insignificant and despised Nazareth would come a seemingly insignificant tender sprout, a *Branch* who would be despised and rejected by men.

Nazareth itself is surrounded by Old Testament history. Within its sight are the battlefields where Barak and Gideon fought victoriously and where kings Saul and Josiah were defeated. It is here where Elijah made his sacrifice to the one true God and where the glorious events of the Maccabean revolt took place. Let's continue hearing about Jesus from the Old Testament perspective.

Continue underlining what you see about the coming Messiah.

Here is my servant, whom I uphold, my chosen one in whom I delight; I will put my Spirit on him and he will bring justice to the nations (Isaiah 42:1, requoted in Matthew 12:18–20).

THE SPIRIT of the Sovereign LORD is on me, because the LORD has anointed me to preach good news to the poor. He has sent me to bind up the brokenhearted, to proclaim freedom for the captives and release from darkness for the prisoners (Isaiah 61:1).

For to us a child is born, to us a son is given, and the government will be on his shoulders. And he will be called Wonderful Counselor, Mighty God, Everlasting Father, Prince of Peace. (Isaiah 9:6)

Rejoice greatly, O Daughter of Zion! Shout, Daughter of Jerusalem! See, your king comes to you, righteous and having salvation, gentle and riding on a donkey, on a colt, the foal of a donkey. (Zechariah 9:9)

2. What relative of Jesus is foreshadowed in the next two passages?

A voice of one calling: "In the desert prepare the way for the LORD; make straight in the wilderness a highway for our God. Every valley shall be raised up, every mountain and hill made low; the rough ground shall become level, the rugged places a plain. And the glory of the LORD will be revealed, and all mankind together will see it. For the mouth of the LORD has spoken." (Isaiah 40:3–5, Matthew 3:3)

"See, I will send my messenger, who will prepare the way before me. Then suddenly the Lord you are seeking will come to his temple; the messenger of the covenant, whom you desire, will come," says the LORD Almighty. (Malachi 3:1)

---

3. Read the following two passages from your Bible and list what you see about the Messiah.

Isaiah 49:1–7

_____

_____

_____

Isaiah 53

_____

_____

_____

_____

_____

_____

The New Testament also instructs us to pay attention to prophecy for direction.

As stated in 2 Peter, we have the word *made more certain* because we have seen prophecy fulfilled in the birth of Christ.

4. Using 2 Corinthians 1:20, fill in the blanks below:

"For no matter how many _____ God has made, they are '_____' in Christ. And so through him the '_____' is spoken by us to the _____ _____ _____."

> *And we have the word of the prophets made more certain, and you will do well to pay attention to it, as to a light shining in a dark place, until the day dawns and the morning star rises in your hearts. (2 Peter 1:19)*

The Old and New Testaments go together, Amen! For every Old Testament promise, there is a New Testament "Yes" in Jesus Christ.

Pause and Apply: How is Jesus the "yes" in your life? Of the above Old Testament descriptors, circle the names for Jesus that you embrace. Conclude with a prayer including the names of Jesus. Here are a few to get you started: Almighty God, Wonderful Counselor, The Resurrection and the Life, Alpha and Omega, The Rock. Praise His Holy Name and thank Him for Who He is.

November 12 The Quiet Obedience of Joseph

Mary is the most recognized person in the Christmas story, but consider the man in the background. Joseph was a person who listened to the Lord and obeyed. What did it take for God to hand over His only Son to an imperfect earthly father? What qualities was God looking for in this adoptive dad? And what was it like for Joseph to consider raising God's perfect Son as His own?

To handle that kind of responsibility, I wonder about Joseph's education. How much did he know about the scriptures before his life was interrupted by an angelic encounter?

Jewish boys were educated in the "house of the book." Their study with a teacher in the synagogue consisted of repeating and memorizing. The length of their education was somewhat dependent on family income. Parents also instructed their children as commanded by Scripture.[16]

Pause and Apply: What if someone instructed you with these words,

> *These commandments that I give you today are to be upon your hearts. Impress them on your children. Talk about them when you sit at home and when you walk along the road, when you lie down and when you get up. Tie them as symbols on your hands and bind them on your foreheads. Write them on the doorframes of your houses and on your gates.*

Someone did. Doesn't it make you demand, "What *are* the commandments? If they're so important, I MUST know them!"

Now that I have your attention, read the commandment that came before.

*Hear, O Israel: The LORD is our God, the LORD is
one. Love the LORD your God with all your heart and
with all your soul and with all your strength.*

There they are, instructions so important Jesus reminds us
of them in the New Testament. Could it be that Joseph's parents took Deuteronomy 6:4–9 very seriously? Perhaps both
Joseph and Mary's parents prepared their children spiritually so
that they could comprehend the fulfillment of Old Testament
scriptures. Perhaps Mary and Joseph then taught these scriptures to their Son Jesus. And perhaps Deuteronomy 6:4–9 is
something we need to consider in our New Testament homes.

Skim Matthew 1:18–25 and Matthew 2 to answer the
following questions.

1. Circle Matthew's focus: Mary or Joseph

2. According to Matthew 1:22, why did all of this take
place?

_____

_____

3. What four significant details are given to Joseph about
the child (verses 20–22)?

_____

_____

_____

_____

4. What does *Immanuel* mean, and how is it still relevant
(verse 23)?

_____

_____

_____

_____

5. In Matthew 2:6–7, the chief priests quote from the Old
Testament and determine where Christ is to be born. Look
back at your November 11th study of prophecy. Where is this
Old Testament prophecy found?

_____

6. What part of this prophecy has been fulfilled?

_____

_____

7. Why did Joseph allow Mary to remain a virgin (Matthew 1:20, 25)?

_____

_____

Now let's travel to Bethlehem Ephratha and see the landscape and its history. Bethlehem lies about 5 miles south and 100 feet higher than Jerusalem at 2,555 feet above sea level. The name Bethlehem may have originated from the word *Lahum* after the Canaanites god of war. The Jews would have changed the name from "house of Lahum" (to make war) to "house of Lahem"(house of bread). From the house of bread would come the *Bread of Life*.[17]

Ephratha meaning *fertility*[18] or *fruitful*[19] certainly fulfills its name! How radically appropriate that Ruth gleans wheat in Bethlehem, the house of Bread, and takes it home to provide for her mother-in-law and herself. In these fields, the Lord blesses Ruth with something better than wheat: Boaz, a Kinsman-Redeemer. Here King David the shepherd king is born, and many years later another Shepherd King is born here—the One called Prince of Peace and Bread of Life, the One who is our Kinsman Redeemer.[20] Joseph may not have fathomed all of this, but Joseph nevertheless followed instructions.

8. Joseph receives four visits and four sets of instructions. Briefly describe each:

Matthew 1:20–21 _____

Matthew 2:13–14 _____

Matthew 2:19–21 _____

Matthew 2:22–23 _____

9. Look closely at Matthew 1:18–25. Why do you think Joseph received most of the instructions?

_____

_____

_____

10. Why was it imperative for Joseph to obey the angel's first and second instructions?

_____

_____

_____

11. What would it take for Joseph to obey these instructions?

_____

_____

_____

Joseph is a man of action, but we are shown few reactions. At least with Mary we hear a question tinged with amazement, "How will this be, since I am a virgin?" And with Zechariah we hear doubting, "How can I be sure of this?" But with Joseph, we have to guess about some of his feelings. The exception is his love for Mary.

To fully understand his commitment to her, we need to understand the Jewish custom of engagement and marriage. Joseph is probably about twenty-four years old, and Mary is about fourteen. If Joseph followed Jewish tradition, he would have researched Mary's parentage, ancestry, and resources, and traced the line of David. He would then have asked her parents if Mary could be his wife. Both sets of parents would have to agree.

At the betrothal ceremony, they sipped from a shared cup of wine, and from that point on the two were legally betrothed. If Joseph died, Mary would be considered a widow. This sacred engagement was basically marriage without living together. Mary and Joseph had celebrated that moment by the time Joseph learned of Mary's pregnancy. A wedding ceremony was still to follow where the two parties would celebrate with decorations of garlands, a gift of jewelry, a veil, attendants, a big feast and marching to music.[21]

After learning of Mary's pregnancy, and knowing he is not the baby's father, Joseph has three choices: to marry Mary anyway, to have her quietly sent away (divorce), or to reveal her situation (adultery), which would result in her stoning.[22]

Joseph no longer wishes to marry her, but he does not want her disgraced or murdered. So he determines to put her away quietly. However, his plans change after the angel explains that the prophecy in Isaiah 7:14 is being fulfilled in Bethlehem. Joseph learns he will be the earthly father of God's Son. From that moment on, we see a man who listens, obeys, and acts. This seemingly background character becomes a major player in the safety of his new family.

If you're curious about the angel Gabriel, you can find him in the Old Testament book of Daniel 8:15–20 and 9:21–26. He is one of only two angels whose names are recorded in Scripture. The other is Michael. Gabriel is always the "special announcement" guy, bringing the big news. It makes me wonder how Gabriel waited out those years between the Old and New Testaments to bring the biggest news of all!

November 13 Zechariah and Elizabeth

Not only do we have a pair of young newlyweds expecting their firstborn son (who also happens to be the Son of God!) but we also have an older couple awaiting the birth of their first and only child, the forerunner to the Son of God.

Both Zechariah and Elizabeth are from a lineage of priests; they are righteous and walk blamelessly. (1 Chronicles 24:1–19 explains the 24 divisions of priests.)

Why Zechariah and Elizabeth have been denied a child up to this point is unclear. Even today, is it ever clear why a wonderful couple is unable to conceive? We all know someone who longs for a child but is unable to become pregnant. The empty void is accompanied by the painful question, "What's wrong with me?" Perhaps the couple even questions why God is denying them a child, especially if having children is their heartfelt prayer.

Women of the Old and New Testaments looked upon childlessness as a curse from God, believing their status to be His punishment. They also felt the barren extinction of the family name. Elizabeth, too, felt the disgrace of never bearing a child.[23] But she couldn't know God's timing and God's bigger picture.

Zechariah's turn to pray in the temple was chosen by lot. But the timing was not by chance or accident, it was a divine appointment.[24] When Zechariah journeyed to the temple to offer the daily sacrifice, this was a once-in-a-lifetime calling—the first and only time Zechariah would enter this holy place. He had probably spent the previous night sleeping near the temple, anticipating the next day's entrance into the sacred place where he would meet with the Most Holy God.[25] Enter God's timing and God's bigger picture.

📖 Read Luke 1:5–20.

1. What can we learn about the background of Elizabeth and Zechariah? (verses 5–6).

_____

_____

_____

2. Why do you think *both* backgrounds are listed?

_____

_____

_____

3. When burning incense and offering his prayers, Zechariah the priest would pray for the nation of Israel and petition for a Messiah. What else do you think Zechariah might have been praying for (Luke 1:13)?

_____

_____

_____

4. When Zechariah is in the tabernacle, an angel appears. Why would this be frightening?

_____

_____

_____

5. Flip back to Genesis to learn about Abraham and Sarah. Read Genesis 13:14–18; 15:4–6; 17:1–7; and 18:10–15. How are the reactions of this couple similar to or different from Zechariah's and Elizabeth's responses?

_____

_____

_____

_____

_____

_____

Sarah's disbelief caused her to engineer a solution which set history on a negative course. God promised a son and would have provided a son in His time, but Sarah could not wait. She gave her servant Hagar to bear Abraham a son. God promised Hagar that her son Ishmael would become a great nation (Genesis 21:18). The conflicts between Abraham's two sons, Isaac and Ishmael, have meant continued conflict and war in the Middle East to this day.

6. What can we learn from Sarah's reactions and actions?

_____

_____

_____

7. While praying, Zechariah heard the angel speak to him. How does God speak to us now? When in prayer, how can we learn to hear God's voice? How do we respond?

_____

_____

_____

_____

_____

_____

Pause and Apply: God has given us many promises. Do we grab hold and claim them or do we wonder if they're really meant for us? Don't be a Zechariah and doubt what God has planned for you. Listen, obey, and claim His promises.

November 14 Song, Symbol, and Suggestion

Song: "O Little Town of Bethlehem"

O Little town of Bethlehem how still we see thee lie
Above thy deep and dreamless sleep the silent stars go by
Yet in thy dark streets shineth, the everlasting light
The hopes and fears of all the years are met in thee tonight

For Christ is born of Mary, and gathered all above
While mortals sleep the angels keep their watch of wondering love
O morning stars together, proclaim the holy birth.
And praises sing to God the king, and peace to men on earth

How silently, how silently, the wondrous gift is given
So God imparts to human hearts the blessings of his heaven
No ear may hear his coming, but in this world of sin
Where meek souls will receive him still, the dear Christ enters in.

O holy Child of Bethlehem, descend to us we pray
Cast out our sin and enter in, be born in us today
We hear the Christmas angels, the great glad tidings tell
O come to us, abide with us, our Lord Emmanuel

For me, some of the most amazing lines of any Christmas carol are found in this carol. Perhaps the most profound line is this one: *The hopes and fears of all the years are met in thee tonight.* After reading the earlier prophecy and knowing how the Jews longed for a Savior that line rings so true!

Where meek souls will receive him still, the dear Christ enters in. Do we have a meek soul? Have we truly received Him? Will we receive Him? The fourth verse says, *Cast out our sin and enter in, be born in us today.* If you've never allowed the Lord to be born in your heart, there is no time like today. Christ will come to us and abide with us, for He is Immanuel—God with us. A God who will meet us wherever we are and stay with us forever.

Perhaps no one understood this better than Phillip Brooks, the lyricist for "O Little Town of Bethlehem" and pastor of Holy Trinity Church in Philadelphia. After President Lincoln's assassination, he was asked to deliver the funeral message. Brooks, an abolitionist, was worn out and discouraged with the Civil War. Needing a time for rest and reflection, he took a sabbatical tour to the Middle East where he experienced Immanuel in a new way.

On Christmas Eve, 1865, Brooks stood in a shepherds' field outside the little town of Bethlehem. As stars twinkled overhead, he experienced an overwhelming feeling of being present at the very first Christmas. Though greatly moved by the emotion of his experience, for many years Brooks was unable to convey it to his congregation. In 1868 he captured the event in a poem that he gave to his organist Lewis Redner. Although inspired, Redner was unable to translate the lines to music.

However, on Christmas Day, Redner awoke with the melody and harmony in his head, calling it a "gift from heaven."[26] That Christmas, when the thirty-six children in Brooks' Sunday school class sang the merging of story and melody, "O Little Town of Bethlehem" was visited once again and born in hearts for Christmases to come. God gave Brooks and Redner a beautiful Christmas gift—a song in their hearts to pass on for generations.

Each time you hear "O Little Town of Bethlehem," put yourself there under the stars, seeing the shepherds and the angels, and the Magi and most of all, the One who meets all the hopes and fears of all the years.

Symbol: Nativity Sets[27]

In the village of Greccio, Italy in 1223, St. Francis of Assisi arranged the first nativity. At an outdoor candlelight mass, the monks from the religious order sang, and townspeople gathered near the manger with candles and torches for a new and inspiring worship experience. Each year this scene is recreated in that same Italian village.

Whether life-size or hand-held, nativity sets still fascinate us. Last Christmas, I wrote a pageant about a group of carolers who vandalize an outdoor nativity set. One caroler remains to meet the elderly owner of the display. As the old man illuminates each nativity figurine, the statue comes to life and relates his story in drama and song. It was my hope that not only would children run to join the nativity characters around the Christ child, but they would forever consider what each character is thinking. After all, isn't that what both children and adults do when we play with individual nativity figurines?

Suggestion 1: Nativity Play

Invite neighborhood children into your home and make little figurines from paper towel rolls or clay. Let them play with the figurines, moving them around as you tell the story. Or purchase inexpensive sets to give as gifts. They can often be found for a few dollars in mail-order catalogs. Remind the children not to put Baby Jesus in the manger until December 25th! Have them start the Magi in the farthest corner of their home and move them closer to the nativity each day of December. Why not sing a few carols including "O Little Town of Bethlehem" as you play with the figurines.

Suggestion 2: Links of Love

My children love to anticipate Christmas by creating a paper chain of red and green links of love. On each link, write down a December activity. Perhaps a picnic dinner of Bethlehem food (pita bread, hummus, dried fruit, yogurt) in front of the fire, or sampling holiday ice cream at the local ice cream parlor. Other Christmas links are acts of service such as making cookies for the fire department, or singing carols over the phone to relatives.

We enjoy preparing our hearts by thinking of what we *can* do, then we anticipate which link will be torn off each day, and finally we put the loving suggestion into action! I've included a list of ideas for these links in the appendix.

Suggestion 3: Advent Wreath

Since Advent is a season of conscious recognition commemorating the arrival of the Messiah, why not light candles to help focus on the many aspects of His coming?

Consider adding a wreath and Advent candles to your dinner table. The circular wreath reminds us that God and His love for us are eternal and have no beginning or end. The greenery represents life. The candles remind us that just as Jesus is the light, we are to be lights to the world.

Begin four Sundays before Christmas Day, usually the Sunday closest to November 30th. The candles for weeks one, two, and four are purple representing royalty. Week three's candle is pink for joy, and the center Christ candle (lit on Christmas Day) is white for purity.

Each week of Advent provides an opportunity to focus on one aspect of Jesus' coming. The weeks may be divided into categories such as hope, love, joy, and peace or the characters in the nativity: prophets, angels, shepherds, and magi, concluding on Christmas Day with Jesus.

Choose your weekly themes, research, and then select a few verses to bring you or your family to the manger by Christmas Day.

Week One:

_____

_____

_____

_____

Week Two:

_____

_____

_____

_____

Week Three:

_____

_____

_____

_____

Week Four:

_____

_____

_____

_____

Christmas Day:

_____

_____

_____

_____

WEEK THREE

Songs of Praise

November 15 Zechariah—One Quiet Husband

When is the baby due? Do you know what you're having? Have you picked out any names? I'm so happy for you! Mothers-to-be constantly hear these comments from well wishers. But consider the comments and the shock in Zechariah's village regarding Elizabeth's pregnancy. Elizabeth and Zechariah were embarrassingly old. Zechariah was mute and Elizabeth was in seclusion, perhaps to wait until the miracle was obvious, or to avoid being Zechariah's sole mouthpiece.[28] Regardless, the two of them don't communicate with others in the usual way for five months or more. I wonder what the villagers were thinking!

Read Luke 1:5–25, Luke 1: 57–80.

1. God has a name picked out for their son, and it's not "Zechariah Jr." The name selected is "John," which means "God is gracious."[29] How is "God is gracious" a fitting choice for Zechariah and Elizabeth's child?

2. What facts are given about Zechariah's child?

_____

_____

_____

_____

_____

_____

_____

3. What prophecy will be fulfilled by John the Baptist? (Malachi 4:6).

_____

_____

While Zechariah prays in the temple, an angel appears, saying Zechariah's prayers have been answered and he'll be a father. Despite the angelic messenger, Zechariah is unconvinced. Questioning Gabriel, "How can I be sure of this?" he asks for a sign. Zechariah's disbelief results in punishment.

4. The angel explains when Zechariah will be able to speak (verse 20). According to Luke 1:63–64, why is this the proper time?

_____

_____

_____

Once again, God's Word proves true. You will see the fulfillment of Old Testament Prophecy as the shepherds find the nativity according to the angel's directions. What God says is always accurate. Believe it. You don't need to ask like Zechariah, "How can I be sure of this?"

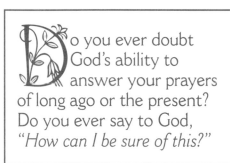

Do you ever doubt God's ability to answer your prayers of long ago or the present? Do you ever say to God, *"How can I be sure of this?"*

And consider this, God is still God whether we believe in Him or not. Our lack of faith does not make God any less; we just fail to experience His power. The Messiah came and Elizabeth had a son with or without Zechariah's immediate faith.

5. When Zechariah comes out of the temple, those waiting realize he has seen a vision because he makes signs but does not speak. Just what kind of signs would Zechariah make to convey an angelic appearance telling him the Messiah was coming and his wife would have a son? Practice your sign language, and try to act out that message!

What did Zechariah "say" to his wife when he got home from work that night? Imagine how he shared the enormity of their situation. Describe that missing scene below.

In verse 62, those around Zechariah are *showing* rather

than *telling* Zechariah what to name his son. When he writes down what the child's name will be, his audience is filled with amazement, fear, and awe. The situation had become the talk of the hill country, with heightened suspense and a captivated audience, ready to ask, "What then is this child going to be?" (verse 66).

At the appropriate time, Zechariah' mouth is opened, and the benediction he should have spoken when he left the temple nine months earlier rushes out.

6. Describe what comes out of Zechariah's heart and mouth (Luke 1:64, 68–79).

_____

_____

_____

Pause and Apply: Whether something good or bad happens, what are the first things out of our mouths? If we paused to utter a response, do you suppose our language would be more uplifting? Maybe sometimes a silent pause is good. What can you praise God for today?

November 16 Zechariah's Song of Prophecy

Zechariah is filled with the Holy Spirit and praises God for who He is, what He is doing, and what He will do. He saved this song in his heart for nine months!

What about us, do we have a song in our heart? Can we go through life singing the praises of God? Today, try singing as you go about your business. Put on a praise CD as you work, drive, or play. Sing God's praises, and let your lyrics be all that God has done in the Bible, or *sing unto the Lord a new song* and praise Him for all He's done in your life. Try one of these Psalms for starters: Psalms 8, 19, 93, 95, 96, 148, 149, or 147.

1. Read Luke 1:67–79, then divide Zechariah's song into verses with titles.

Zechariah's Song:

1_____

2_____

3_____

2. Who is the *horn of salvation* (verse 69)?

_____

In Psalm 18:2, we read about the horn of David's salvation.

The LORD is my rock, my fortress and my deliverer;
my God is my rock, in whom I take refuge. He is my
shield and the horn of my salvation, my stronghold.

The horn is a symbol of light, strength, glory and power, of a kingdom, and an altar of refuge and safety—all descriptions of Jesus.

3. In Zechariah's song, how many times is salvation listed?

_____

4. What other words are repeated?

_____

5. If you have cross-references in your study Bible, can you determine how many times Zechariah quotes from the Old Testament?

_____

6. Why is Zechariah able to prophesy (verse 67)?

_____

_____

7. What specifics do we learn about Jesus from this song of prophecy?

_____

_____

_____

8. In verses 76 and 77, Zechariah describes John. Fill in the blanks below: "And you, my child, will be called a _____ of the Most High; for you will go on _____ the Lord to _____ the _____ for him, to give his people the _____ of _____ through the _____ of their _____."

The first chapter of the Gospel of John also describes John the Baptist.

9. Underline words from John 1:6–8 that correspond with Zechariah's prophecy. How do these scriptures from the book of John confirm Zechariah's prophecy?

_____

_____

_____

_____

John later introduces himself; "I am the voice of one calling in the desert, 'Make straight the way for the Lord' " (John 1:23). John the Baptist refers to the Old Testament, knowing he is the New Testament Elijah prophesied about in Isaiah 40:3.

> *There came a man who was sent from God; his name was John. He came as a witness to testify concerning that light, so that through him all men might believe. He himself was not the light; he came only as a witness to the light.* (John 1:6–8)

When you see the connections between Old and New Testaments, doesn't it make your heart beat a little faster? God connects us so completely to what He has done in the past, what He is doing in the present, and what He will do in the future. We need to understand and see how we're part of His plan. We, too, can *make straight the way of the Lord.*

Pause and Apply: In what ways have you seen *past* experiences prepare you for the *present*, and perhaps for *future* ministry? How can you *make straight the way* for someone else to know the Lord? How do you feel God's gentle tugging?

November 17 Mary and the Angels

Mary is indeed one of the most beloved characters in the Christmas story. Today we'll meet this special young lady right when the angel first greets her.

📖 Read Luke 1:26–38.

1. How many months after Gabriel visits Zechariah does he visit Mary?

_____

2. Write the words the angel uses to address Mary.

_____

_____

How would you receive this greeting?

_____

_____

3. According to verses 29 and 30, how did Mary react?

_____

_____

The King James Version reads, "She was troubled at his saying, and cast in her mind what manner of salutation this should be" (Luke 1:29). The Greek word for *troubled* is *diatarasso,* meaning "to agitate greatly." The root word *dia* means "throughout."[30] With this description we can better understand the level of her discomfort.

She handles her anxiety by *casting in her mind.* The word for casting is *dialogizomai—dia* meaning "through," and *logizomai,* "to reason." Thus, she *reasoned through.*[31]

4. What two separate comments does the angel repeat?

_____

_____

_____

5. What qualities in Mary might have found favor with God?

_____

_____

_____

6. From verses 31–34 list all the information Mary is given about her child.

_____

_____

_____

7. What are three reactions Mary could have had?

_____

_____

_____

_____

_____

_____

Ultimately, this could have been Mary's death sentence. Adulterers and women pregnant out of wedlock were often stoned to death. Mary doesn't appear to be disturbed about her fate. But could she fully understand the work God had begun in her? Philip Yancey writes,

> The God who came to earth came not in a raging whirlwind nor in a devouring fire. Unimaginably, the Maker of all things shrank down, down, down, so small as to become an ovum, a single fertilized egg barely visible to the naked eye, an egg that would divide and re-divide until a fetus took shape, enlarging cell by cell inside a nervous teenager.[32]

8. Mary does have a question for the angel. She knows she's a virgin, so how could she be pregnant (Luke 1:34)? How do Mary and Zechariah's questions differ (Luke 1:18)?

_____

_____

_____

_____

9. After her initial question, what is Mary's ultimate position (verse 38)?

_____

_____

10. The power of the Most High *overshadowed* Mary. Who is the Father of Mary's Son (verse 35)?

_____

11. Why do you think Mary is given the additional information that Elizabeth has also conceived (verse 36)? Did the angel specifically tell her to make haste to Elizabeth's house?

_____

_____

_____

What seems impossible in your life—something that only God could solve? In what areas do you need to claim verse Luke 1:37?

12. Why do you think Mary would travel 50–79 miles to the hill country while pregnant?

_____

_____

_____

13. Luke 1:37 is an amazing verse. Why is this crucial to the entire Bible—to creation, salvation, resurrection, and this mysterious virgin birth?

_____

_____

_____

14. We see a huge fast-forward between verses 55 and 57. I'd love to read the "expanded version," if one existed. We know Mary stayed with Elizabeth for three months, went home, and Elizabeth gave birth to John. I just wonder what went on for those three months? What do you think may have happened during this time?

_____

_____

_____

_____

15. Read Colossians 1:15–18 and underline all attributes of Jesus. After reading these details, how would you feel being Jesus' mother?

_____

_____

_____

Pause and Apply: The baby in the manger is the image of the invisible God, the firstborn over all creation as well as the Creator. He holds all things together. He is the head, the first, the beginning —"so that He Himself might come to have first place in everything" (Colossians 1:18b [NASB]). Does He have first place in your life? When you pray to Him, can you even begin to comprehend the power of Jesus' name?

> *For God was pleased to have all his fullness dwell in him, and through him to reconcile to himself all things, whether things on earth or things in heaven, by making peace through his blood, shed on the cross.* (Colossians 1:19–20)

November 18 Mary and Elizabeth

Have you and a friend ever gone through a significant life event at the same time? Perhaps you've shared a graduation, new career, engagement, or marriage. If you've ever been pregnant, did you confide in someone during the nine months? If you've adopted a child, did you find other adoptive parents to share the struggles and joys as you awaited your child?

A close friend and I both longed to have babies. We agonized over the wait. However, one day she announced she was pregnant, and the very next week, I discovered I was, too. We commiserated about nausea, predicted the sexes of our children (with 50% chance of being correct, we were both wrong), and shopped for baby supplies. Sharing the excitement doubled our anticipation.

Can you imagine how Mary hungered to share with the older relative, and soon-to-be first time mom, who was also a part of this amazing plan? How wonderful it must have been for the two to share these miraculous secrets. Let's see the reunion between these two women chosen by God.

Read Luke 1:39–56.

1. Before Mary left Nazareth, whom do you think she told of her pregnancy or of Elizabeth's?

_____

_____

2. Do we have any information about whether Mary explained her pregnancy to Elizabeth?

_____

_____

3. How might Mary's friends and family in Nazareth have reacted to her pregnancy?

_____

_____

_____

4. From verse 36, what two things does Mary actually know about Elizabeth's pregnancy?

_____

_____

_____

> *In a loud voice she exclaimed; "Blessed are you among women, and blessed is the child you will bear! But why am I so favored, that the mother of my Lord should come to me? As soon as the sound of your greeting reached my ears, the baby in my womb leaped for joy. Blessed is she who has believed that what the Lord has said to her will be accomplished!"* (Luke 1:42–45)

Elizabeth may have needed companionship and conversation as well. She must have yearned to know more about her miraculous pregnancy. Is it any wonder that when Elizabeth exclaims to Mary, she does so in a *loud* voice (verse 42)?

5. What purpose could Mary's presence have had in Elizabeth's life?

_____

_____

_____

6. When Elizabeth hears Mary's greeting, two things happen:

_____

_____

_____

7. How is what happened to Elizabeth a fulfillment of Luke 1:15?

_____

_____

_____

8. Why would Elizabeth's baby have that type of reaction to Mary's voice (verse 41)?

_____

_____

_____

9. In verse 43, what does Elizabeth call Mary's baby?

_____

Mary's hasty departure for Elizabeth's home in the hill country included no quick telephone call, no cell-phone interaction on the way, no e-mailing, and probably not even a letter saying she was coming. This makes Elizabeth's declaration all the more miraculous. We almost expect Mary to say, "But Aunt Elizabeth, how could you *know*? I never *told* you *that!*"

10. Consider Elizabeth's salutation in verses 42–45. How might Mary feel to be addressed this way by an older relative?

Somehow Elizabeth knows Mary believes the Word of God, *"Blessed is she who has believed that what the Lord has said to her will be accomplished!"* (Luke 1:45). Is it evident to others that you believe God's Word? Does God's love shine through what you say and do?

_____

_____

_____

11. How could Elizabeth know Mary believed the Word from God (verse 45)?

_____

_____

_____

12. The following statements are true about one or both of the women. Mark "M" for Mary or "E" for Elizabeth next to the statements that are true for that person. Mark "B" next to the statements that are true for both.

- ■ Some will consider the pregnancy a disgrace
- ■ Some will rejoice that this previously barren woman's disgrace is removed
- ■ Humble
- ■ Low economic and social standing

- Wife of obscure, country person
- From unnamed village in hill country
- Stigma of childlessness
- Stigma of pregnancy before marriage
- Very young
- Very old
- From lineage of Abraham and David
- From lineage of the tribe of Abijah
- Described as righteous
- Virgin
- Married for many years
- Knows she's pregnant with a son
- Favored
- Surprised by pregnancy
- A part of a glorious miracle
- Revealing the miracle will cause great joy
- Revealing the miracle will cause suspicion

Mary and Elizabeth are two very different women, and yet both women share a secret which the world cannot understand. Nevertheless, these two women react to God's pronouncements with great joy.

Pause and Apply: No matter what our circumstances, we, too, can be filled with the Holy Spirit and rejoice in God's plan for our relationship with Him and others. Connect with someone around you. Send a note to a new acquaintance, phone a lonely neighbor, visit someone who is housebound. Share a piece of yourself and find common ground. If you're not in a circle of believers, come back into fellowship with other sisters in the Lord.

November 19 Mary's Song

The Gospel of Luke treats us to the songs and speeches of Zechariah, Simeon, Elizabeth, the angels, and Mary. Immediately after Elizabeth's blessing, Mary praises God. We've read Zechariah' song; today let's look at Mary's.

📖 Composers from Monteverdi to Bach to Mozart have taken this text and composed beautiful songs of hope and joy called *Magnificats*. Begin your day by reading aloud this song of praise from Luke 1:46–55.

1. From this song, what can you can deduct about Mary's knowledge of the Bible?

_____

_____

_____

2. Try dividing the Song of Praise in two. What would you title verses 46–50?

_____

What could you label verses 51–55?

_____

3. Look up the following Old Testament scriptures and note similarities with Mary's song. Jot down the New Testament verse numbers from Mary's Magnificat, which match the Old Testament scriptures below.

Genesis 17:19

1 Samuel 2:1

1 Samuel 2:7

Psalm 35:9

Psalm 98:1

Psalm 103:17

Psalm 118:15

Psalm 132:11

4. How many verses from Mary's Magnificat are about Mary and her particular situation? _____ How many of the verses are about God? _____

How many verses are about her Son?_____

What can we conclude about her focus of praise?

_____

_____

_____

5. To exult in praise, what must be true of Mary's spiritual life?

_____

_____

6. What does Mary claim God has done? List at least five things (verses 46–55).

_____

_____

_____

_____

_____

Mary's song of praise is not about baby booties and decorating her Son's room in camel-and-donkey wallpaper. Instead, Mary looks forward to all her Son will accomplish for His people. She praises God for what He has done, is doing, and will do. We could do the same.

hat or Who is the focus of your praise?

Pause and Apply: Do we recognize what God has done for us in our past and throughout history so we're able to sing a song of praise? If this is tough for you, try praising God's character, His promises, and all He will do in the future. Keep this in mind as we enter the season of Thanksgiving.

November 20 Songs of Hannah, Zechariah, and Mary

Mary and Zechariah's New Testament songs of praise have many similarities. Zechariah prayed alone in the holy temple. After his son was born and his lips were unsealed, he uttered a benediction of praise. We don't know whether Mary prayed to be the mother of God's Son, but she was chosen, and so, magnified the Lord in praise.

Now let's look at Hannah's song from the Old Testament. Hannah was a childless woman who longed for a baby (see 1 Samuel 1) and perhaps prayed in front of a congregation of worshipers at the house of the Lord. Her prayers were answered, and like Zechariah and Mary, she prayed a song of praise to God.

Read these three songs and note the similarities and differences by circling similarities, and using arrows or just plain scribbling to note the differences between the three passages. You're allowed to make a mess!

Hannah

1 Samuel 2:1–10

Then Hannah prayed and said:

My heart rejoices in the LORD; in the LORD my horn is lifted high. My mouth boasts over my enemies, for I delight in your deliverance. There is no one holy like the LORD: there is no one besides you; there is no Rock like our God. Do not keep talking so proudly or let your mouth speak such arrogance, for the LORD is a God who knows, and by him deeds are weighed. The bows of the warriors are broken, but those who stumbled are armed with strength. Those who were full hire themselves out for food, but those who were hungry hunger no more. She who was barren has borne seven children, but she who has had many sons pines away. The LORD brings death and makes alive; he brings down to the grave and raises up. The LORD sends poverty and wealth; he humbles and he exalts. He raises the poor from the dust and lifts the needy from the ash heap; he seats them with princes and has them inherit a throne of honor. For the foundations of the earth are the LORD'S: upon them he has set the world. He will guard the feet of his saints, but the wicked will be silenced in darkness. It is not by strength that one prevails; those who oppose the LORD will be shattered. He will thunder against them from heaven; the LORD will judge the ends of the earth. He will give strength to his king and exalt the horn of his anointed.

Zechariah

Luke 1:67–79

His father Zechariah was filled with the Holy Spirit and prophesied:

Praise be to the Lord, the God of Israel, because he has come and has redeemed his people. He has raised up a horn of salvation for us in the house of his servant David (as he said through his holy prophets of long ago), salvation from our enemies and from the hand of all who hate us—to show mercy to our fathers and to remember his holy covenant, the oath he swore to our father Abraham: to rescue us from the hand of our enemies, and to enable us to serve him without fear in holiness and righteousness before him all our days. And you, my child, will be called a prophet of the Most High; for you will go on before the Lord to prepare the way for him, to give his people the knowledge of salvation through the forgiveness of their sins, because of the tender mercy of our God, by which the rising sun will come to us from heaven to shine on those living in darkness and in the shadow of death, to guide our feet into the path of peace.

Mary

Luke 1:46–55

And Mary said:

My soul glorifies the Lord and my spirit rejoices in God my Savior, for he has been mindful of the humble state of his servant. From now on all generations will call me blessed, for the Mighty One has done great things for me—holy is his name. His mercy extends to those who fear him, from generation to generation. He has performed mighty deeds with his arm; he has scattered those who are proud in their inmost thoughts. He has brought down rulers from their thrones but has lifted up the humble. He has filled the hungry with good things but has sent the rich away empty. He has helped his servant Israel, remembering to be merciful to Abraham and his descendants forever, even as he said to our fathers.

November 21 Song, Symbol, and Suggestion:
"Something Sweet"

Song: "Angels We Have Heard on High"

Angels we have heard on high sweetly singing o'er the plains
And the mountains in reply echoing their joyous strains
Gloria in excelsis Deo.

Shepherds, why this jubilee why your joyous songs prolong?
Say what may the tidings be, which inspire your heav'nly song?
Gloria in excelsis Deo.

Come to Bethlehem and see Him whose birth the angels sing;
Come, adore on bended knee Christ the Lord, the newborn King.
Gloria in excelsis Deo.

See within a manger laid, Jesus, Lord of heav'n and earth!
Mary, Joseph, lend your aid, With us sing our Savior's birth.
Gloria in excelsis Deo.

As a singer, "Angels We Have Heard on High" is one of my favorite carols because of its glorious, meandering, eighteen-note melisma on the word *Gloria!* This song can make any singer sound great even without the echoing chamber of a shower stall!

"Angels We Have Heard on High" is an early carol. The use of Latin and the simplicity of the vocal line suggest it originated as a chant taught by a monk or priest. The first verse tells the story of Jesus' birth from the shepherds' perspective; the second from perhaps a curious Bethlehem resident asking why the shepherds are so happy. The third is the shepherds' answer, urging them—or perhaps all of us—to come to Bethlehem to adore the newborn King. And finally we arrive and "see within a manger laid" the one who is Lord not only of earth but also of heaven. I especially appreciate the inclusion of Mary and Joseph who must have been quite surprised by their shepherd visitors and the story they share. They are invited to join in singing "Gloria!"

Between each verse, we are the angel choir beautifully floating with the descending line, "Glory to God in the highest!" or *Gloria* ("glory") *in excelsis* ("in the highest") *Deo* ("God"). The Glory of God is brought down to the lowly shepherd and to all of us.

Symbol: The Candy Cane[33]

According to legend, there was a choirmaster at the Cologne Cathedral around the year 1670 who wanted the children in his Christmas service to listen and learn. After devising a sweet silencer and lesson plan, he asked the local confectioner to design a piece of stick candy bent on one end. The shape allegedly represented the shepherd's crook, and the white color stood for Christ's purity.

Over the years, derivations of this candy followed. Red stripes were added many years later. Some say the many thin stripes represent the stripes Christ received when whipped by Roman soldiers before His crucifixion.

And the refreshing flavor? Of course no one knows for sure why mint was chosen for the candy cane. But, we do know that mint (hyssop) is associated with purification, cleansing, and sacrifice in the Old Testament. When we think of the minty flavor of the candy cane, we are reminded that Jesus is pure. He cleanses us from sin; and He was the perfect sacrifice.

The candy cane's texture? Hard as a rock, and Jesus is indeed the Rock. Other legends about the candy cane suggest that the upside down hook is the letter "J" for Jesus.

The candy cane remains a Christmas favorite and sweet distraction for any happily-ever-after kind of celebration.

Suggestion: Peppermint Bath Salts

I don't know of a woman who doesn't need a little pick-me-up in December. We love indulging our senses in the smells of Christmas, and we also love feeling warm and appreciated. Combine these loves into one hospitality gift; peppermint bath salts for your visitors.

Purchase epsom and rock salts. Mix the salts together in a large bucket (4 to 1 ratio epsom to rock or sea salt) and add drops of peppermint oil. Pour half the mixture in another bucket. To one bucket add natural red food coloring. Stir the bucket. Now you have one bucket of reddish-pink peppermint salts and one bucket of white.

Using a funnel, pour the rock salt into baby food jars, alternating red and white until you have a peppermint-striped design. Tie a red ribbon around the neck of the jar. Prepare a card including the candy cane information. Personalize the card by writing,

Treat yourself to a hot bath.

Wake up with the scent of peppermint

and remember:

I care about you and so does God!

Punch a hole in the card and tie it to the jar. If you want to get fancy, add a peppermint candy cane and an envelope of hot chocolate—a complete bath time escape!

If your friend prefers showers to baths, there are plenty of peppermint options.

- Candy cane ornaments made out of flour, salt, water, and food coloring paste.
- Peppermint Fudge
- White chocolate bark swirled with crushed peppermint
- Decorate your doorframe with a length of cellophane-wrapped candy canes.
- Tie a gold jingle bell and red and green ribbons between each link.
- Let guests snip off a jingle and sweet treat as they leave.

Believers in Action

November 22 Always Thanksgiving

Though we're studying Christmas, it's still Thanksgiving season. Thanksgiving is sandwiched between the candy of Halloween and the presents of Christmas; and because it is non-commercial, giving thanks does not receive the emphasis it deserves.

> *The LORD is my strength and my shield; my heart trusts in him, and I am helped. My heart leaps for joy and I will give thanks to him in song. (Psalm 28:7)*

But today we'll be like Hannah, Zechariah, and Mary and stop to praise God and thank Him for all He has done.

Pause and Apply: Prepare your heart for Thanksgiving by writing your own prayer or song of praise. Here are a few ideas to get you started.

1. Start by opening your Bible to the book of Psalms.

2. Read Psalms 138, 145, or 147. If you have children, read Psalm 136 and for every remembrance, they can echo, *"His love endures forever!"* Or create your own remembrances, listing God's faithfulness in the life of your family; then let your children echo *"His love endures forever"* from Psalm 136.

3. Recall Old Testament Bible stories.

4. Consider the names given for Jesus and God.

5. Prepare your heart for Thanksgiving by writing your own song or prayer of praise and thanksgiving. What has God done in your life? Dedicate this praise to Him. Be brave and read it as your prayer at Thanksgiving dinner. You'll be surprised how uplifting it is, and how it magnifies the Lord.

First Thessalonians 5:16–18 says, "Be joyful always; pray continually; give thanks in all circumstances." By remembering the words "always," "continually," and "in all circumstances," we can make Thanksgiving a yearlong holiday.

November 23 Our Messiah is Born!

At last the long awaited moment arrives. The time is full. All prophecy will be fulfilled and filled full with the birth of Jesus. This is the moment cited in Galatians 4:4–5.

Let's follow Mary and Joseph from Nazareth to Bethlehem. On this five day, eighty-mile journey, the two journeyed from verdant Galilee through bleached Samaria and the hills of Judea. They traveled past the Mount of Olives and Gethsemane, never comprehending this area would be where their son's life would both begin and end.

Mary may have walked. Women were subservient and often followed behind their husbands. Or Mary may have ridden with her head veiled, sitting sideways on the donkey, a bag of food on the other side. Either way, it could not have been comfortable to leave family and friends to travel so near her delivery date.

Mary and Joseph may have arrived in Bethlehem in late afternoon or evening when all lodging rooms were taken. The town was indeed little—with a population of between one hundred to three hundred residents. Consider Bethlehem's one main street, crowded with villagers and foreigners forced into registering to pay taxes to a greedy ruler. Consider Mary and Joseph's disappointment at finding no room in the inn. The inn may have been a portion of a home or a large temporary shelter erected to house the overflow in crowded times.[34]

Perhaps Mary and Joseph knew they were fulfilling prophecy by journeying to Bethlehem, but they couldn't know their Son would be born in a lowly stable. Although we often depict that stable as an A-frame nativity set, it was probably one of the many dark caves dotting the hills around Bethlehem, often used by shepherds and animals.[35]

The cave did not look like our Italian Renaissance-style nativity sets. It was dirty and dark. The initial smell of an enclosed area with little fresh air would have hit them hard. They may have longed for better footwear to handle the layers of manure caked on the floor of a cave not recently mucked. Above their heads, the ceiling may have been stained with soot from the shepherds' many fires.[36]

> *But when the time had fully come, God sent his Son, born of a woman, born under law, to redeem those under law, that we might receive the full rights of sons.* (Galatians 4:4–5)

The crude manger was probably a feeding trough with sweet smelling, possibly containing old chewed oats and the remainder of a salt cake at the bottom. And the animals? Though perhaps not all the animals depicted in decorative nativity sets, some of God's creation probably surrounded Mary and Joseph.

And what about the birth itself? Who delivered the Son of God? Midwives usually assisted in delivering, and husbands were not allowed to help. Did young Mary deliver her own child? That's pause for thought!

And what about God? Philip Yancey writes,

How did God the Father feel that night, helpless as any human father, watching his son emerge smeared with blood to face a harsh, cold world? Lines from two different Christmas carols play in my mind. One, 'The Little Lord Jesus, no crying he makes,' seems to me a sanitized version of what took place in Bethlehem.[37]

Now, with a realistic picture of Mary and Joseph's surroundings, let's visit the manger, near the newly born Son of God, by reading Luke 2:1–20.

1. Remember the Old Testament prophecy found in Micah 5:2? How does this prophetic utterance reappear in Luke 2:4?

_____

_____

_____

2. Why did Mary travel to Bethlehem so near her delivery date?

_____

_____

_____

3. Verses 6–7 indicate *whose* firstborn son?

_____

So popular are the words to "Away in a Manger," there are at least three lullaby tunes that contain the familiar lyrics to this song. However, this simple carol is not just for a baby, it's for all of us who want to come to Jesus like children, entering an eternal relationship with Immanuel.

Be near me Lord Jesus, I ask Thee to stay,

Close by me forever, and humbly I pray.

Bless all the dear children in Thy tender care.

And fit us for heaven to live with Thee there.

4. According to Luke 2:9–12, who were the first ones to hear the good news? Why they?

_____

_____

_____

5. I always pictured an instantaneous *crowd* of angels. However, initially, there was only *one* angel appearing to shepherds who are surrounded by God's glory. Why would God begin with just one angel?

_____

_____

_____

6. What would it feel like to be a simple shepherd surrounded by the glory of God?

_____

_____

_____

Philip Yancey speculates on the contrast in *The Jesus I Never Knew*.

> For just an instant the sky grew luminous with angels, yet who saw that spectacle? Illiterate hirelings who watched the flocks of others, "nobodies" who failed to leave their names. Shepherds had such a randy reputation that proper Jews lumped them together with the "godless," restricting them to the outer courtyards of the temple. Fittingly, it was they whom God selected to help celebrate the birth of one who would be known as the friend of sinners.[38]

7. What was the initial reaction of the shepherds?

_____

_____

_____

8. What were the first words the shepherds heard?

_____

9. In contrast to fear,
What is offered?

_____

How will we feel?

_____

_____

_____

To whom is it offered?_____

10. Compare Luke 1:11–13 with Luke 2:9–12. What is similar about Zechariah and the shepherds' angelic encounter?

Zechariah's angelic encounter surprised and frightened him. Though the angel spoke good news designed to bring cheer, a fearful Zechariah asked for a sign.

The shepherds were also surprised, frightened, and told not to fear. They were offered Good News and then given a sign, although they didn't ask for one. Zechariah and the shepherds came from completely different religious backgrounds and locations, yet the shepherds were ready to act on the good news.

11. Verse 11 reveals many roles for Jesus: Savior, Christ, and Lord. How do these names reveal different aspects of Him?

Savior: Deliverer, Preserver

_____

_____

_____

Christ: Anointed, Messiah

_____

_____

_____

Lord: Having Power or Authority[39]

_____

_____

_____

12. Why do the shepherds need a sign (verse 12)?

_____

_____

_____

13. What joins the Angel?

_____

14. What is the multitude's reaction to *God on earth*?

The Greek word for angel is *angelos,* the Hebrew is *malak;*[40] both meaning "messenger." These ranks of angels function not only as messengers but divine protectors. Angels are described as created beings which number in the millions and are mentioned over three hundred times in the Bible. There are forty-five encounters mentioned in the Old Testament and seventy appearances in the New.

What do angels look like? Seraphim and cherubim have wings. But what did Zechariah, Mary, Joseph and the shepherds actually see? In most church Christmas pageants, angels are little children wearing white robes and silver halos. Ironically, these little cherubs are often the ones needing to be told, "Fear Not!"

The only angelic description we have is that the angel was accompanied by the glory of the Lord shining around the shepherds. Oh, to be in that field on that amazing night! What an evening for this group of shepherds! God had come to earth as a baby and sent His angels (whatever they look like) to tell them the good news.

How should the angel's statement reassure us today (verses 10–11)?–Remember, we are the *all people* and we have been given *good news* and *great joy,* and we are to *fear not!* We need to live with confidence the good news of Christmas.

November 24 Shepherds in Action

The shepherds clearly know what to do with the good news. They react and then act! Re-read Luke 2:8–20 and consider the following:

1. What was the shepherds' reaction to the news and their subsequent action (verses 15–17)?

_____

_____

_____

2. From whom do the shepherds believe the information came (verse 15)?

_____

3. How do the shepherds find the place where Jesus was born? Do you think they had any trouble?

_____

_____

_____

_____

> ome to the manger;
> fall on your knees,
> Come to the manger,
> there you'll find peace
>
> Come to the manger, see
> God's little boy
>
> Come to the manger, experi-
> ence joy
>
> Come to the manger, find
> others to bring
>
> Come to the manger, worship
> the King
>
> Come to the manger, see
> God's gift from above
>
> Come to the manger, the
> manger of love[41]

4. How would Mary and Joseph feel after hearing what was revealed to the shepherds (verses 17–19)?

_____

_____

_____

5. Write below the portion of the angel's statement matching what the shepherds find.

_____

_____

_____

6. Verse 18 says "all who heard it. . . ." Who might that include?

_____

_____

7. Those who heard it were amazed. They were awe-struck by what they were told. In contrast, Mary's reaction in verse 19 is prefaced with "But Mary treasured. . . ." How are _pondering_ and _treasuring_ different from _wondering_ (verse 18)?

_____

_____

Mary kept all the information safe and close within her; she cast her thoughts together and reflected upon them. She gathered all the pieces of the story together in the very center of her being.

Consider the shepherds. They heard the good news, but they didn't keep it to themselves. They shared it with Mary and Joseph as well as anyone who listened to them as they left the nativity. What about us? Do we hoard the good news of Jesus' birth, or do we share it with others?

10. What relationship do the shepherds have with God after they leave the manger?

_____

_____

11. God gave Mary plenty of confirmations of His presence and His plan. To review, consider how many confirmations Mary received regarding her pregnancy. First an angel spoke to her. Second, Elizabeth revealed information only the Holy Spirit could have revealed to Elizabeth. Third, Joseph shares that an angel spoke to him regarding Mary's pregnancy.

Add three more divine confirmations as you read on in the next few days.

1. Angel
2. Elizabeth
3. Joseph
4.
5.
6.

Can you imagine the excitement of hearing pieces of confirmation about God's plan? Consider your favorite mystery. Characters convene to decipher clues and connect dots. The excitement mounts as each character reveals new details, remembrances, and fragments of information. Mary and Joseph must have experienced that sense of awe as they heard and saw the information pieced together, revealing the big picture of God's incredible plan.

As a person who wonders about the details, I'm curious about a few missing scenes. I wonder about the days in the stable. How long did Mary, Joseph, and baby Jesus remain in a dark cave before moving into better housing? How long was Jesus wrapped in swaddling clothes? (The common belief at the time was that binding a baby's arms tightly to his side would keep a child's limbs straight and firm.)[43] Who brought food to Mary and Joseph? Where did they eventually reside?

Pause and Apply: As we conclude today, consider Mary and her quiet peace. Mary was a teenage mom without a layette or crib. Mary did not have the luxury of friends and family bringing her a few weeks' worth of hot meals. And yet we do not read about her "stressing out." Rather, we see Mary pondering and treasuring. What was the source of her peace? What can we learn from Mary?

Can we plan a quiet place and reserve a special time each day of December to ponder and treasure this amazing story? Pour a cup of hot tea, bring your Bible, and meet Jesus there.

November 25 The Christmas Story

I cannot listen to the Christmas story without reflecting on *A Charlie Brown Christmas* and hearing little Linus quote the familiar text. Read Luke 2:1–20 aloud to yourself or others in your home. If you have children, encourage them to act out the story, put on a puppet show, or move the nativity set figures around. Even if you don't have children, become a child at heart and dramatize Christmas!

One year I directed a church Christmas pageant entitled "O Little Town of Leesburg." It explored what would have happened if Jesus had been born in our hometown two thousand years later. Although it felt unusual presenting the familiar Christmas story in a nontraditional setting, finding a way to dramatize it was a great way to get to the heart of its meaning.

This year, you're the writer and director. You've been asked to take your favorite scene from Luke's Christmas story.

1. Describe which scene you'd choose and how you'd bring it to life. List your dream cast of actors and actresses.

_____

_____

_____

_____

_____

_____

2. Considering the prophecies you've studied, the line of individuals it has taken to arrive at this birth, and the many characters of the Nativity, what do you personally find most intriguing?

_____

_____

_____

3. Consider what question you would ask each character.

Mary

_____

_____

Joseph

_____

_____

Shepherd Boy

_____

_____

Elizabeth

_____

_____

Zechariah

_____

_____

Herod

_____

_____

Do we praise God for what we've seen and heard and how it aligns with Scripture? Or do we know the scriptures well enough to *be able* to praise God for His consistency and revelation? What promises do we need to understand so that we can marvel at God's ways?

5. In the movie version of *Luke's Christmas Story,* which part would you want to play?

_____

6. What do you know this Christmas that you didn't know last Christmas?

_____

_____

_____

_____

Pause and Apply: In *The Jesus I Never Knew,* author Philip Yancey asks himself, "If Jesus came to reveal God to us, then what do I learn about God from that first Christmas?"[44] What an appropriate question. How would *you* answer it?

> *No one has ever seen God, but God the One and Only, who is at the Father's side, has made him known.* (John 1:18)

After over thirty years on earth, Jesus Himself explains, "I am the way and the truth and the life. No one comes to the Father except through me. If you really knew me, you would know my Father as well. From now on, you do know him and have seen him" (John 14:6–7). He further adds, "Anyone who has seen me has seen the Father" (verse 9) and "I am in the Father and the Father is in me" (verse 11).

What do you know about God after seeing God explained or made known in Christ?

_____

_____

_____

November 26 Simeon: A Man Who Waited to See God

Remember our study of Old Testament Messianic prophecy? What if you had been given the *prophecy* as well as the *promise* that you would meet the Messiah? Today we'll look at a man blessed with both.

When Jesus was eight days old, he was circumcised according to Old Testament instruction and given the Hebrew name

Jeshua meaning "The Lord is Salvation." When we use the name *Jesus*, we are using the Greek and Latin translation.[45] Jesus was named by His Father in heaven. God knew the importance of His name, and the plan for Jeshua's life.

Forty days after His birth, Joseph and Mary then took the five-mile, two-hour journey to the temple in Jerusalem where they offered a burnt offering in accordance with scripture.

First read Luke 2:21–24, and then read the Old Testament scriptures below for historical background.

Exodus 13:1–2, 14–15
Leviticus 12:2–8
Numbers 18:15–16

List what must happen, according to these scriptures:

_____

_____

_____

_____

1. On the eighth day, the boy is to be _____ _____ (Leviticus 12:3).

2. When the days of her purification are over, she is to bring to the priest at the entrance to the Tent of Meeting a _____for burnt offering, and _____ or _____for a sin offering (Leviticus 12:6).

3. The Priest presents the offering before the _____ (Leviticus 12:7).

4. If the parents are too poor, then two_____ or two_____ are offered. (Leviticus 12:4–8)

When Mary and Joseph offer a sacrifice, it is not a lamb. What can we deduce about them?

_____

_____

_____

5. The first son must be _____ at _____ shekels (Numbers 18:15–16).

📖 Read Genesis 17:1–14.

6. With whom did circumcision begin (verse 10)?

_____

7. What was the meaning of circumcision (verse 11)?

_____

_____

_____

8. List five aspects of God's covenant with Abraham (verses 5–8).

_____

_____

_____

_____

_____

> When you were dead in your sins and in the uncircumcision of your sinful nature, God made you alive with Christ. He forgave us all our sins, having canceled the written code, with its regulations, that was against us and that stood opposed to us; he took it away, nailing it to the cross.
> (Colossians 2:13–14) 🎵

📖 Now read the New Testament verses from Colossians 2:11–14 on circumcision.

After reading Colossians 2:11–14, can you hear the hammers pounding the nails into the cross? By those nails, we have been freed from death and freed from the code!

9. Luke 2:22 says that Joseph and Mary took Jesus to Jerusalem to present him to the Lord. What would it mean to present God's Son to the Lord, His Father?

_____

_____

_____

Consider for a moment that in Matthew 3:16–17 after John the Baptist baptizes an adult Jesus, we see the heavens open, the Spirit of God descend like a dove, and we hear the words from God: "This is my Son, whom I love; with him I am well pleased." We hear these words again at the transfiguration (Matthew 17:5). And 2 Peter 1:17 reiterates that Jesus "received honor and glory from God the Father when the voice came to him from the Majestic Glory, saying, 'This is my Son, whom I love; with him I am well pleased.'" Though we don't hear the words at His birth, God must have loved seeing His Son in the temple.

10. How are God's Old Testament instructions to Moses (printed below) uniquely fitting for Jesus?

> The LORD said to Moses, "Consecrate to me every firstborn male. The first offspring of every womb among the Israelites belongs to me, whether man or animal." (Exodus 13:1–2)

> You are to give over to the LORD the first offspring of every womb. All the firstborn males of your livestock belong to the LORD. (Exodus 13:12)

> *(as it is written in the Law of the Lord, "Every first-born* MALE THAT OPENS THE WOMB SHALL BE CALLED HOLY TO THE LORD"). (Luke 2:23 NASB)

_____

_____

Since the Passover, when God preserved all of the Jewish firstborn males, all firstborn males have belonged to God. Parents paid five shekels to the priest to redeem their child. Was it necessary for Mary and Joseph to do this? Jesus already belonged to God. He *was* and *is* God. How interesting to present Him *holy* before God! He *was* and *is* Holiness.

Now let's meet someone who has been waiting for Jesus. Mary and Joseph's encounter with Simeon is another confirmation from the Lord. You can add Simeon to the list of people who confirmed God's plan.

Read Luke 2:25–35.

11. What four descriptions are given of Simeon?

_____

_____

_____

_____

_____

_____

12. What was unusual about Simeon?

_____

_____

13. What was Simeon's focus in life?

_____

In *One Incredible Moment*, Max Lucado describes Simeon's looking as "waiting forwardly."

> Of all the forms of *look*, the one that best captures what it means to "look for the coming" is the term used to describe the action of Simeon: *prosdechomai*. *Dechomai* meaning "to wait." *Pros* meaning "forward." Combine them and you have the graphic picture of one "waiting forwardly." The grammar is poor, but the image is great. Simeon was waiting; not demanding, not hurrying, he was waiting.[46]

Simeon didn't seem to need an introduction to His Savior. He knew Truth when he saw Him. Can we claim the same? Can we say, "For my eyes have seen your salvation!"?

14. When Simeon entered the temple, he was ready to see someone. What prepared him for what he saw? How did he know to go into the temple at that particular time?

_____

_____

_____

15. Do we have any indication of Simeon's age? What's your guess? Why do we imagine that age?

_____

_____

16. Simeon also proclaims why Jesus has come. Who does he list first?

_____

17. Why would Mary and Joseph be amazed and marvel at the things being said about Jesus?

_____

_____

Simeon prophesies that Jesus will be a "sign that will be spoken against" (Luke 2:35). In this usage, the word "sign" is indicative of a "warning or admonition."[47] But when the angel told the shepherds "This will be a sign to you" (Luke 2:12), "sign" meant something that "distinguished a person or thing from others."[48] Indeed, the babe wrapped in swaddling clothes and lying in a manger would be spoken against and crucified for what distinguished Him from all others.

18. How do you think Mary felt about Simeon's prophecy in Luke 2:35? Once again, we see the crucifixion foreshadowed. Do you think Mary understood the meaning of the words?

_____

_____

Mary is forewarned that her soul will be pierced through. I wonder if she felt dread or apprehension at that warning. Could she understand what was to come?

The Greek word translated "soul" is *psuche*, which means "breath of life."[49] A mother's "breath of life" would be pierced as she stood beneath a cross, helplessly watching her son die. Nothing Simeon prophesied could have ever prepared her for that moment.

> "And a sword will pierce your own soul too." (Luke 2:35b)

19. Simeon was righteous and devout. He was no doubt a man who knew the Scriptures. Of what benefit were they to him? Why do we, like Simeon, need to be prepared with the Scriptures?

_____

_____

_____

One benefit of being prepared with the scriptures is that in the midst of a battle we are reminded of the One who is victorious. Philip Yancey writes about Simeon's convictions.

> "Somehow Simeon sensed that though on the surface little had changed—the autocrat Herod still ruled, Roman troops were still stringing up patriots, Jerusalem still overflowed with beggars—underneath, everything had changed. A new force had arrived to undermine the world's powers."[50]

When we look at our list of characters, some, like the shepherds and magi, are not given specific names. Although he appears in but a few verses, Simeon plays a specific role and is named, perhaps so he will be an example for all to remember.

Pause and Apply: Simeon was looking forward to the Messiah. He had something wonderful to wait for. What do you look forward to in life? Is it temporal or is it eternal? Simeon causes me to consider what I anticipate right now. "The consolation of Israel" (Luke 2:25) was one of the one hundred or so names for the Messiah. Is He *your* hope and comfort?

As we consider New Year's Resolutions, perhaps we should remember how Simeon knew the scriptures and looked forward to seeing Jesus. Almost everything I look forward to will come and go, but Jesus is eternal. Looking forward to spending time with Him now prepares me for eternity. We, too, could pray to be filled with the Holy Spirit, and to lead lives of righteousness and devotion.

November 27 Anna, A Woman Who Waited to See God

Not only did God reveal the Messiah to a man in the temple, but God showed His Son to Anna, a woman from the tribe of Asher. Like Simeon, she is named, but the Bible records few verses about her. According to the description given, Anna is between the ages of 84 and 104 years of age. She is a woman who truly awaited the revelation of God's promise.

Read Luke 2:36–40 and enjoy her inclusion, though brief, in the Christmas story.

1. According to verse 36, what are Anna's qualifications?

_____

_____

_____

2. Where did Anna live (verse 37)?

_____

3. How often did she serve in the temple? And what did she do there? How many years might she have done this?

_____

_____

_____

4. How does Anna recognize Jesus?

_____

_____

5. In what two ways does Anna respond (verse 38)?

_____

_____

_____

6. Anna's reaction was two-part. How do we respond when we recognize all God has done for us? What actions can you take today in response to your faith in Jesus?

_____

_____

_____

> *She never left the temple but worshiped night and day, fasting and praying. Coming up to them at that very moment, she gave thanks to God and spoke about the child to all who were looking forward to the redemption of Jerusalem. (Luke 2:37–38)*

Pause and Apply: God had a plan for His Son's life well before He named Him Savior. God has a plan for the lives of all His children and we can be a part of it through backyard Vacation Bible Schools, children sermons, or volunteering in the nursery. What a privilege to teach children who might grow up to be an Anna or a Simeon.

God chose Mary and Joseph to be the parents for His only Son, looking beyond their financial status. Two turtledoves, a sacrifice costing about sixteen cents, reveal that Mary and Joseph were very poor. But God knew what counted in training up a child: faith, trust, and obedience. Mary and Joseph had a loving commitment to one another, to their child, and to dedicating their child to God. They followed the scriptures for direction. Verse 39 says that at Jesus' presentation, Mary and Joseph did everything required by the law of the Lord. Their lives had a plan and a purpose.

Like Mary and Joseph we need to dedicate our children to the Lord. We need to pray that they grow strong in the Lord, guide them to understand His grace, and instruct them in the Word so they are filled with His wisdom. We need to teach our children about Jesus' birth, death, and resurrection so that they call on the name Jesus' heavenly Father gave Him.

Circle the words that reveal the position of Jesus' name. Underline what should happen at the pronouncement of His name.

> *And the child grew and became strong; he was filled with wisdom, and the grace of God was upon him.* (Luke 2:40)

> *Therefore God exalted him to the highest place and gave him the name that is above every name, that at the name of Jesus every knee should bow, in heaven and on earth and under the earth, and every tongue confess that Jesus Christ is Lord, to the glory of God the Father* (Philippians 2:9–11).

This common and ordinary name has extraordinary powers. Praise the name of Jesus, the name above all names!

November 28 King Herod and the Magi

Anna and Simeon looked forward to seeing Christ. They did not fear him; they longed for his arrival. However, King Herod feared Him and did not long for His arrival.

In a story so full of contrasts: palace and cave, shepherds and Magi, humans and angels, we now have King Herod the Great contrasted with the great King of the Universe. *Herod the Great, Jesus the King: The True Christmas Story* featuring historian Ray Vander Laan is a wonderful video detailing these contrasts.

Every good story needs an antagonist, and Herod takes that role. At Christmas, it's not pleasant to read about violence, but knowing what happened helps us understand the angel's warnings and the subsequent movements of other key players in the story.

So, if he's so bad, why is he called Herod the *Great*?

Herod ruled Judea, often with vision and strong political instincts, from 37 BC until his death in 4 BC. Though not a kind person, he was, at times, politically great and politically correct with Rome's hierarchy fifteen hundred miles away. Herod was also known for the impressive architecture he constructed with Jewish labor. His own multi-storied, fortress-like palace called the *Herodium,* sat on a hill overlooking the region.[51]

But Herod's personal life was a mess. Frankly, Herod appears to have been an unscrupulous, ruthless monster. He married ten times—with one of these marriages being into a royal Jewish family. He called for the execution of his uncle, mother-in-law, beloved wife Mariamme, father-in-law, his three sons: Antipater, Aristobulus, and Alexander, his barber, and a close friend. Additionally, he had the high priest and his brother-in-law drowned.[52]

In Herod's regime, executions were rampant. Five days before Herod died, he arrested three thousand of Jerusalem's respected citizens, giving orders for them to be executed upon his death. He wanted to ensure people mourned on the day of his death—even if it wasn't for him.[53]

Now you can see the significance of the Magi's avoiding Jerusalem and Herod's questions on their return trip. Their caution allowed time for Mary, Joseph, and Jesus to flee to Egypt, a ten-day journey, twice the distance from Nazareth to Bethlehem. God's warning dream instructed Joseph to flee with his family. Here we see another example of an Old Testament passage with an additional layer of meaning when referenced in the New Testament. "WHEN ISRAEL was a child, I loved him, and out of Egypt I called my son" (see Hosea 11:1; Matthew 2:15).

Herod the "not-so-great" had not forgotten about the prophesied birth and was furious. In order to wipe out any chance a new baby would eventually rival his power, he destroyed all children in the region two years of age and under—including his own son. Though death toll estimates range from two hundred to two thousand, it is more realistic to estimate thirty to sixty children in a village of three hundred. Losing one tenth of Bethlehem's population would have meant extreme grief and mourning.[54]

When you read Matthew 2:1–23 again, note that verse 18 refers to the Old Testament passage of Jeremiah 31:15, which describes the grief among the Israelites when they were taken as captives to Babylon. Matthew, because of his Jewish background and audience, incorporated ninety-three quotes from the Old Testament. This is yet another example of how Old Testament prophecy can be pertinent both to the time in which it was written and to future events as well.

> "A voice is heard in Ramah, weeping and great mourning, Rachel weeping for her children and refusing to be comforted, because they are no more."
> (Matthew 2:18)

Believe it or not, a Christmas carol describes Herod's horrible deed. Set in a minor key, this haunting lullaby, with words from a song written in 1534, is titled "Lully, Lullay," but is often called "Coventry Carol." The song originated in Coventry, England, where the local crafts guild performed a pageant depicting Herod's slaughter and the subsequent sorrow. During the pageant mothers sing the children to sleep with "Lully, Lullay" so Herod's soldiers can't find them. The words themselves sound like a mother lullying her baby to sleep.

Lully, Lullay

Lully, thou little, tiny child
By, by lully, lullay
Lully, Thou little tiny Child
By, By, Lully, Lullay

O sisters, too, how may we do for to preserve this day
This poor young ling for whom we sing
By, By, Lully, Lullay

Herod the King in his raging, charged he hath this day
His men of might, in his own sight, all children young to slay.

Then woe is me, poor Child, for Thee, and ever mourn and say
For thy parting, nor say, nor sing,
By, By, Lully, Lullay.

Read Matthew 2:1–12 to answer the following questions.

1. What was Herod's reaction when he heard about the King of the Jews (verse 3)?

_____

_____

2. Who else was frightened (verse 3)?

_____

3. Whom did Herod call together (verse 4)?

_____

4. Has Herod spoken with the Magi yet? How does he eventually call for them? (verse 7).

_____

_____

_____

5. Why would Herod want to know when the star appeared to the Magi? What would this tell him about the child?

_____

_____

_____

Pause and Apply: Bethlehem was about six miles from Herod's palace. What kept Herod from checking it out himself? Are there times in our lives when we, too, have more fear than faith; more doubt than love? Do we ever know the truth, but have trouble embracing it? Do we watch others travel toward Christ while we stay behind? What about those who heard in Jerusalem? What kept them from checking out the birth of a King?

If you've found yourself frustrated, angry, doubting, or apathetic, then now is the best time to turn everything over to God. He knows you, loves you, and wants to bless you with His peace and joy.

November 29 The Mystery of the Magi

The first six words of "We Three Kings" hold at least three fallacies: they were *Magi* not kings; their number is unknown; and they were not from the Orient. The Magi came from the east, a journey of a thousand miles, anywhere from Arabia, Media, or, most likely, Persia. Although there is so much we do not know about the Magi, we do know this: they were wise; they knew the prophecy and were acting on it; they brought gifts; and they recognized the greatness of the Lord.

By current definition, astronomy focuses on the scientific aspects of the "laws and movements of the stars,"[55] whereas astrology searches for meaning in those movements and attempts to interpret them. We view these as distinctly different studies. However, in Jesus' time, astronomy and astrology were combined. In other words, stargazers such as the Magi were looking at laws and movement, but also for interpretation.

The Magi's practice was sometimes considered a prestigious profession combining science and religion. They could also have been specialists in medicine, religion, divination, magic, philosophy, or mathematics. They may have been followers of Zoroastrianism, but much is left to speculation.[56]

So where did the term "We Three Kings" come from? Perhaps the connection comes from the messianic prophecy found in Psalm 72, which refers to an Old Testament King but foretells that Jesus is the ultimate King. Verses 10–11 speak of kings presenting gifts. Underline all words and phrases that might be prophetic.

The Kings of Tarshish and of distant shores will bring tribute to him; the kings of Sheba and Seba will present him gifts. All kings will bow down to him and all nations will serve him.

Long may he live! May gold from Sheba be given him. May people ever pray for him and bless him all day long. (verse 15)

Similarly, Isaiah 60 sheds light on the coming Light of the world and those who brought gifts.

ARISE, SHINE, for your light has come, and the glory of the LORD rises upon you. See, darkness covers the earth and thick darkness is over the peoples, but the LORD rises upon you and his glory appears over you. Nations will come to your light, and kings to the brightness of your dawn. (Isaiah 60:1–4)

Herds of camels will cover your land, young camels of Midian and Ephah. And all from Sheba will come, bearing gold and incense and proclaiming the praise of the LORD. (Isaiah 60:6)

We've become increasingly familiar with the depiction of kings in regal robes because medieval and Renaissance painters reveled in painting the royal figures. We've locked in three as the "magi" number because three presents were offered to the Christ child and literature named them Caspar, Balthazar, and Melchior.

After peeling away the painted layers of kingly fairytale, what remains? What should we believe about these men from the east? Our assumptions, and the Magi's past practices, should not reduce our awe of how God used them. They were philosophic astrologers and wise-enough men to seek the one true King. God used them to expand the Christmas story to distant lands and to remind us that not only was the good news of the Messiah given to poor, lowly shepherds, but to these wealthy and learned non-Jews. The Magi gave of their time, money, and energy to find the King and to bow down and worship Him. They are an example for everyone.

Read about the Magi account in Matthew 2.

1. Do we know if the Magi visited the palace on their own initiative or if they were summoned once they arrived in Jerusalem?

_____

_____

2. What did Herod call Jesus (verses 4, 8)?

_____

What did the Magi call Jesus, and why did they want to find Him (verse 2)?

_____

_____

_____

Why would this alarm Herod?

_____

_____

_____

3. When the Magi quoted Old Testament scripture (Micah 5:2) in verse 6, what was Jesus called?

_____

Both Herod's and the Magi's use of names revealing Jesus' power, *King of the Jews* and *Christ*

> "Where is the one who has been born king of the Jews? We see his star in the east and have come to worship him." (Matthew 2:2)
>
> " 'But you, Bethlehem, in the land of Judah, are by no means least among the rulers of Judah; for out of you will come a ruler who will be the shepherd of my people Israel.' " (Matthew 2:6)

("Anointed One," "Messiah"), show they believed Jesus was somebody special. However, while Herod felt threatened by the King of the Jews, the Magi worshiped the baby. What a contrast! Herod and the Magi recognize, perhaps even believe, but while the Magi bowed down, Herod became enraged and destroyed lives. When Jesus Christ later hung on the cross, He was identified as *King of the Jews, Christ,* and *King of Israel,* but it didn't mean those uttering the titles truly believed and accepted Him (Mark 15:26, 30–32, Luke 23:39).

5. Why did Herod claim he wanted the report of the Christ child? What was his true motive?

6. What five actions did the Magi take (Matthew 2:9–12)?

_____

_____

_____

_____

_____

7. Why didn't the Magi return to Herod (verse 12)? How did God speak to the Magi?

_____

_____

_____

8. Why did Joseph return to Nazareth (verses 22–23)?

_____

_____

9. How did God speak to him (verse 22)?

_____

10. God warned in dreams. How does he warn us now?

_____

_____

_____

11. We don't bring gold, frankincense, and myrrh, but what *do* we bring the Lord?

_____

_____

_____

12. What does Matthew 2:9–10 say about the activity of the star? "And the star they had seen in the east went _____them until it _____over the place where the _____ was."

Pause and Apply: Many have tried to explain the "star of wonder" which guided the Magi to the young King. Was it a comet, the planet Venus, a supernova, a conjunction of planets, a pause in planetary orbit, or perhaps even Halley's Comet, which actually appeared in approximately 12 BC. A star hovering over the birthplace of the Son of God was definitely supernatural.[57]

But then again, given all the other amazing miracles in the Christmas story, why does a supernatural occurrence created by God seem so contrived? After all, "He determines the number of the stars and calls them each by name" (Psalm 147:4). Couldn't the God who created and placed the stars in the sky also create a star of wonder to lead a group of mathematicians away from their past and toward a glorious new hope in Christ? After all, God led the Israelites with a pillar of fire by night and a cloud by day toward their Promised Land! What would be so difficult about creating a single star to guide seekers to the Perfect Light?

> On coming to the house, they saw the child with his mother Mary, and they bowed down and worshiped him. Then they opened their treasures and presented him with gifts of gold and of incense and of myrrh.
> (Matthew 2:11)

Star of Wonder, Star of Light.
Star with royal beauty bright.
Westward leading, still proceeding,
Guide us to Thy perfect light.

November 30 Song, Symbol, and Suggestion: "Threes"

Song: "We Three Kings"

John Henry Hopkins was a brilliant scholar, an Episcopal Priest, and a reporter for a New York paper. Hopkins either wrote "We Three Kings" for a Christmas pageant or as an Epiphany gift for his nieces and nephews.

Regardless of its origins, "We Three Kings," with its Middle Eastern flavor, minor key, and 3/4 time became a truly unique Christmas present for all children and a gift that keeps on giving in church pageants everywhere.

Symbols: Gold, Frankincense, and Myrrh

Gold was even more valuable in Jesus' time than it is now. Gold was given only to someone of importance. The only *child* who ever received gold? A King. The Magi honored Jesus' kingship with their gift of gold. The gold was practical and precious and may have helped fund Mary and Joseph's flight to Egypt.[58]

Frankincense and Myrrh, both resins extracted from trees, are collected in a process similar to how we gather maple syrup. The bark is stripped, the wood cut, then the tree's wound bleeds. The resins' distant location and difficulty of production make the supply of frankincense and myrrh very limited and valuable.

Frankincense is an antiseptic, anti-fungal, and anti-inflammatory substance made from a plant from East Africa and the Northern part of the Arabian Peninsula. The plant itself has clear green leaves and pretty star-shaped pink flowers with yellow centers. God instructed the use of frankincense as sacred incense in the temple or the Tent of Meeting. Burning incense is associated with meeting God and offering up prayers to Him.[59]

Myrrh is found in Somalia, Ethiopia, and Arabia and comes from a pale yellow shrub with a large trunk and knotted branches. Myrrh also has antiseptic and analgesic properties. This aromatic orange-colored resin provides the scent for anointing oils, perfumes and embalming liquids, hence the reference to the *gathering gloom*. When Jesus died, His body was anointed with myrrh as a part of the burial process (John 19:39).[60]

Consider again the three verses of "We Three Kings." The three gifts honored Jesus as King, High Priest, and victor over

> "Born a King on Bethlehem's plain, Gold I bring to crown Him again,
>
> King forever, ceasing never Over us all to reign"
>
> (Verse 2 from "We Three Kings")

> *Frankincense to offer have I, Incense owns a Deity nigh*
>
> *Prayer and praising all men raising, Worship Him, God on High*
>
> (Verse 3 from "We Three Kings")

death. Did the Magi understand the meaning behind their gifts? Jesus did not write out his Christmas wish-list. Did God tell the Magi what to bring? The gifts could have gone unnamed, but instead Matthew listed each, causing us to speculate!

Thankfully, we are not left with the stone cold tomb of the fourth verse. The final verse exclaims the Easter part of our Christmas celebration.

Glorious now behold Him arise, King and God and Sacrifice;

Alleluia! Alleluia! Sounds through the earth and skies

> *Myrrh is mine, its bitter perfume*
>
> *Breathes a life of gathering gloom,*
>
> *Sorrowing, sighing, bleeding, dying,*
>
> *Sealed in the stone-cold tomb*
>
> (Verse 4 from "We Three Kings")

Suggestion 1: Three Gifts

Some families reduce the clutter of Christmas and the stress of shopping by giving only three gifts to one another. In an article from *Christian Parenting Today*,[61] Trina Conner Schaetz creatively enhances this idea. She suggests exchanging three gifts: a gift of gold, a gift of frankincense, and a gift of myrrh.

The gold present is something the recipient has always wanted and should be wrapped in gold paper. The frankincense gift should remind the recipient to meet with God (a Christian book or CD) and is wrapped in white. The myrrh gift can be bath beads, soaps, lotions, shampoo, shaving cream, or anything that prepares the body and reminds the heart that Christ's significance extends beyond the manger. Wrap the myrrh gift in dark paper. While Christmas celebrates birth, the story is not complete without the reminder that Christ was born to die and rise again.

Another threesome gift idea is to give one prized, one practical, and one gift of time—such as a pair of tickets to an event to be shared with the giver. Planning three gifts, simplifies shopping and increases creativity. Best of all, the recipient considers each gift more special and memorable.

Suggestion 2: Giving a Gift to Jesus

We give to others, but, like the little drummer boy, often have no gift to bring the Christ Child. What does He desire from you this season? Write on slips of paper what would please Jesus—more time with Him in prayer, helping a needy neighbor, loving a difficult person. Put each slip in a box and wrap it. On Christmas Day, unwrap the gift to Jesus and try to live out these gifts in the coming days and weeks.

This completes our November study. Now we'll continue in the Word with thirty-seven days of short devotions through January 6th. Each day you'll read a scripture, reflect on your November study, and conclude with a starter prayer that begins but leaves room for you to continue talking to Immanuel. Add your own Amen!

Spend your December rejoicing over the Good News! Fall on your knees as you meet your Messiah—Immanuel, God with *you;* and experience a Christmas like no other.

November Bible Study Endnotes

Week 1

1. *Encyclopedia of the Bible*, ed. John Drane, (Oxford, England: Lion Publishing, 1998), 238–239.

2. *The Lion Encylopedia of the Bible*, ed. John W. Drane, David Field, Alan Millard, 2nd ed., (Batavia, Illinois: Lion Publishing), 1978.

3. Joseph J. Walsh, *Were They Wise Men or Kings? The Book of Christmas Questions* (Louisville, KY: Westminster John Knox Press, 2001), 122–123.

4. Philip Yancey, *The Bible Jesus Read* (Grand Rapids, MI: Zondervan, 1999), 212.

5. Paul L. Maier, *In the Fullness of Time: A Historian Looks at Christmas, Easter, and the Early Church* (Grand Rapids, MI: Kregel, 1991), 24.

6. Yancey, *The Jesus I Never Knew* (Grand Rapids, MI: Zondervan, 1995), 38.

7. John D. Clare, Henry Wansbrough, *The Bible alive: Witness the Great Events of the Bible* (London, England: HarperCollins, 1993), 126.

8. *Ryrie Study Bible, New American Standard Translation,* (Chicago, IL: Moody Press, 1976), 1542.

9. *Nelson's Complete Book of Bible Maps and Charts* (Thomas Nelson: 1996), 329.

10. Clare, Wansbrough, 126.

11. Maier, 342; "Questions and Answers: 'Is Mary's Lineage in One of the Gospels?'" http://www.bible.org/qu.asp?topic_id=55&qa_id=61/; Bob Deffinbaugh, Th.M, "The Origins of Jesus Christ (Matthew 1:1–25)," *Studies in the Gospel of Matthew,* http://www.bible.org/page.asp?page_id=1034/

12. Ace Collins, *Stories Behind the Great Traditions of Christmas* (Grand Rapids, MI: Zondervan, 2003), 70–75; Walsh, 23–24.

13. Family Life Today, "Adornaments." These can be purchased at www.fltoday.org and 1-800-FL-Today.

Week Two:

14. Bob Deffinbaugh, Th.M, "The Origins of Jesus Christ (Matthew 1:1–25)," *Studies in the Gospel of Matthew,* http://www.bible.org/page.asp?page_id=1034/

15. John D. Davis, Henry Snyder Gehman, *Westminster Dictionary of the Bible* (Philadelphia, Pennyslvania: Westminster Press, 1898, 1944), 36; Craig, S. Keener, *The IVP Bible Background Commentary: The New Testament* (Downers Grove, IL: InterVarsity Press, 1993), 51.

16. Ralph Gower, *The New Manners and Customs of Bible Times* (Chicago, IL: Moody, 1987), 83–85.

17. J. Hampton Keathley, III, Th.M., "Acclamations of the Birth of Christ (Luke 2:1–20)," http://www.bible.org/page.asp?page_id=982/

18. *Harper's Bible Dictionary*, ed. Paul J. Achtemeier (San Francisco: Harper & Row, 1985), 273.

19. *Ryrie Study Bible, New American Standard Translation* (Chicago, IL: Moody Press, 1976), 1387.

20. Keathley, III, http://www.bible.org/page.asp?page_id=982/

21. Paul L. Maier, *In the Fullness of Time: A Historian Looks at Christmas, Easter, and the Early Church* (Grand Rapids, MI: Kregel, 1991), 17, 20.

22. Ibid., 21.

23. Deffinbaugh, "The Silence is Shattered (Luke 1:1–38)," in *Luke: The Gospel of the Gentiles,* http://www.bible.org/page.asp?page_id=1006/

24. W. E. Vine, Merrill F. Unger, William White, Jr., *Vine's Complete Expository Dictionary of Old and New Testament Words* (Nashville, TN: Thomas Nelson, 1984), 381.

25. Beth Moore, *Jesus the One and Only* (Nashville, TN: LifeWay Press, 2000), 4.

26. Dale V. Nobbman, *The Christmas Music Companion Fact Book* (Anaheim Hills, CA: Centerstream Publishing, 2000), 56.

Week Three:

27. Joseph J. Walsh, *Were They Wise Men or Kings? The Book of Christmas Questions,* (Louisville, Kentucky: Westminster John Knox Press, 2001), 29–30; Ace Collins, *Stories Behind the Great Traditions of Christmas* (Grand Rapids, MI: Zondervan, 2003), 138–43.

28. Bob Deffinbaugh, Th.M, "The Silence is Shattered (Luke 1:1 38)," in *Luke: The Gospel of the Gentiles,* http://www.bible.org/page.asp?page_id=1006/

29. *Ryrie Study Bible,* New American Standard Translation (Chicago, IL: Moody Press, 1976), 1545.

30. W. E. Vine, Merrill F. Unger, William White, Jr., *Vine's Complete Expository Dictionary of Old and New Testament Words* (Nashville, TN: Thomas Nelson, 1984), NT: 644.

31. Ibid., NT: 91.

32. Philip Yancey, *The Jesus I Never Knew* (Grand Rapids, MI: Zondervan, 1995), 36.

33. Ace Collins, *Stories Behind the Great Traditions of Christmas* (Grand Rapids, MI: Zondervan, 2003), 41–45; Lori Walburg, *The Legend of the Candy Cane* (Grand Rapids, MI: Zonderkidz, 1997); Jane Jarrell, Mary Beth Lagerborg, *Great Books to Read and Fun Things to Do with Them* (Grand Rapids, MI: Zondervan, 2000), 128–30; Winifred Walker, *All the Plants of the Bible* (Garden City, NY: Doubleday & Company, Inc., 1979), 96–97.

Week Four:

34. Ralph Gower, *The New Manners and Customs of Bible Times* (Chicago, IL: Moody, 1987), 240.

35. Paul L. Maier, *In the Fullness of Time: A Historian Looks at Christmas, Easter, and the Early Church* (Grand Rapids, MI: Kregel, 1991), 32.

36. Ray Vander Laan & Focus on the Family Video, *Herod the Great, Jesus the King: The True Christmas Story, That They May Know* (Grand Rapids, MI: Zondervan, 1999).

37. Yancey, *The Jesus I Never Knew*, 42.

38. Ibid., 37.

39. Vine, 548, 101, 379.

40. Ibid., NT: 26, OT: 4.

41. Ann Stewart, "Come to the Manger, A Children's Christmas Pageant," 2004.

42. W. E. Vine, Merrill F. Unger, William White, Jr., *Vine's Complete Expository Dictionary of Old and New Testament Words* (Nashville, TN: Thomas Nelson, 1984), NT: 395, 340, 476.

43. *Harper's Bible Dictionary*, ed. Paul J. Achtemeier (San Francisco: Harper & Row, 1985), 62.

44. Yancey, *The Jesus I Never Knew*, 35–36.

45. *Ryrie Study Bible, New American Standard Translation* (Chicago, IL: Moody Press, 1976), 1445.

46. Max Lucado, *One Incredible Moment* (Nashville, TN: J. Countryman/Thomas Nelson, 2001), 38.

47. Vine, 575.

48. Ibid., 575.

49. Ibid., 588.

50. Yancey, *The Jesus I Never Knew*, 33.

51. Vander Laan & Focus on the Family Video (video production).

52. Joseph J. Walsh, *Were They Wise Men or Kings? The Book of Christmas Questions*, (Louisville, KY: Westminster John Knox Press, 2001), 44–45; Daniel B. Wallace, Th.M., Ph.D., "The Birth of Jesus Christ," http://www.bible.org/pageg.asp?page_id=656/; Deffinbaugh, "Two Incredible Journeys (Matthew 2:1–23)," in *Studies in the Gospel of Matthew*, http://www.bible.org/page.asp?page_id=1054/; Deffinbaugh, "Responses to the Revelation of the Coming of the King (Matthew 2:1–12, 16–18)," http://www.bible.org/

53. Deffinbaugh, "Two Incredible Journeys Matthew 2:1–23."

54. Deffinbaugh, "Christmas Faith (Matthew 1:18—2:23)," http://www.bible.org/page.asp?page_id=670/; Maier, 64; Daniel B. Wallace, Th.M., Ph.D., "The Birth of Jesus Christ," http://www.bible.org/pageg.asp?page_id=656/

55. Deffinbaugh, "Two Incredible Journeys (Matthew 2:1–23)."

56. Maier, 48–50; *Nelson's Illustrated Encyclopedia of Bible Facts*, ed. J. I. Packer, Merrill C. Tenney, William White, Jr. (Nashville, TN: Thomas Nelson Publishers, 1995), 147.

57. Deffinbaugh, "Two Incredible Journeys Matthew 2:1–23"; Maier, 51–61; Walsh, 40–41.

58. Deffinbaugh, "Two Incredible Journeys (Matthew 2:1–23)"; "Responses to the Revelation of the Coming of the King (Matthew 2:1–12, 16–18)," http://www.bible.org/

59. Winifred Walker, *All the Plants of the Bible* (Garden City, NY: Doubleday & Company, Inc., 1979), 78–79.

60. Ibid., 122–123.

61. Trina Conner Schaetz, "Searching for Myrrh." *Christian Parenting Today* (Fall 2002), 31–32.

Sources for Christmas Carol Research

The sources for the carol research are listed below, except for a few instances when I've made more specific references in endnotes.

Ace Collins, *Stories Behind the Best-Loved Songs of Christmas* (Grand Rapids, MI: Zondervan, 2001).

Ernest K. Emurian, *Living Stories of Famous Hymns* (Grand Rapids, MI: Baker, 1955).

Christopher Idle, *Christmas Carols and Their Stories* (Batavia, IL: Lion Publishing Corporation, 1988).

Dale V. Nobbman, *The Christmas Music Companion Fact Book.*

The New Oxford Book of Carols, Hugh Keyte and Andrew Parrott, eds. (New York: Oxford Press, 1992).

Virginia Reynolds, *The Spirit of Christmas: A History of Best-Loved Carols* (White Plains, NY: Peter Pauper Press, Inc., 2000).

Preparing My Heart for Advent

DEVOTIONS FOR DECEMBER AND THE NEW YEAR

December 1—The Joy of Every Longing Heart

Light: *May God himself, the God of peace, sanctify you through and through. May your whole spirit, soul and body be kept blameless at the coming of our Lord Jesus Christ. The one who calls you is faithful and he will do it* (1 Thessalonians 5:23–24).

Reflection:

My children aren't allowed to ask "How many days until Christmas?" until December 1st. Once December *first* arrives, I have to answer that question. It's a little like the "When will we get there?" question that comes from my two little girls on any car trip lasting over fifty minutes. Although I tire of answering the question, anticipation can be positive. Advent is a time to wait, anticipate, and prepare our hearts for the coming of Jesus.

"Come, Thou Long Expected Jesus" is a carol about the Israelites' longing for a Savior. They wanted someone to free them from fears, sins, and ultimately, they wanted someone to give them a much-needed rest. The carol could be subtitled "Simeon's Song," for he, too, longed for consolation and hope.

But maybe the song is really for all of us. We, too, long to be set free from our fears. We need to be forgiven. And oh, how we need rest! We need Jesus, who says, "Come to me, all you who are weary and burdened, and I will give you rest. Take my yoke upon you and learn from me, for I am gentle and

My children aren't allowed to ask "How many days until Christmas?" until December 1st.

humble in heart, and you will find rest for your souls" (Matthew 11:28–29).

As we prepare for Jesus' birthday, we need to stop and remember that He is our consolation, our strength, our hope, and most definitely the "joy of every longing heart."

Charles Wesley's lyrics in "Come Thou Long Expected Jesus" remind us that Advent is a time to celebrate Jesus' coming to earth, His coming to reign in our hearts, and His future second coming, when we will be raised to His glorious throne to live with Him forever. And that, my friend, is the best part of Christmas! With a hope like that, it's easy to see why it's so important to celebrate Advent. Christmas is one day, but Advent anticipates eternity.

> As we prepare for Jesus' birthday, we need to stop and remember that He is our consolation, our strength, and the "joy of every longing heart."

"Come, Thou Long Expected Jesus"

Come, Thou long expected Jesus,
Born to set thy people free;
From our fears and sins release us,
Let us find our rest in Thee.
Israel's Strength and Consolation,
Hope of all the earth Thou art;
Dear desire of every nation,
Joy of every longing heart.
Born thy people to deliver,
Born a child and yet a King.
Born to reign in us forever,
Now Thy gracious Kingdom bring.
By Thine own eternal Spirit,
Rule in all our hearts alone;
By Thine all-sufficient merit,
Raise us to thy glorious throne.

Response: *Lord Jesus, You were born a child and yet a king. May You be my consolation, hope, and strength as I focus on You throughout the holidays. Help me to see Your birth with its eternal perspective, for one day, I, too will be raised up to live with You forever.*

December 2—Keeping your Eyes on Perfection

Light: *You will keep in perfect peace him whose mind is steadfast, because he trusts in you. Trust in the LORD forever, for the LORD, the LORD, is the Rock eternal* (Isaiah 26:3–4).

Reflection:

Our historic Virginia church on Main Street was packed with parents and visitors eager to watch the annual Christmas pageant. After weeks of rehearsals, my preschool and elementary cast of shepherds, wise men, angels, and stable animals were ready to perform. Or so I hoped.

The pageant began with a nervous fourth grader narrating, "And a decree went forth from *Sy uh REE uh. . . ,*" she said, struggling with the pronunciation. We all felt her hesitation, including a preschooler dressed as a nativity rooster who belted out, *"DY-uh-ree uh?"* Giggles resounded from the rest of the preschool barnyard of sheep, donkeys, roosters, and cows. The audience nervously joined in the laughter. That was only the beginning.

Things got worse when the angels began fighting in the balcony. Prior to the performance, my assistant director suggested that because the kindergarten and first grade angels were unsure of their song, I should have my daughter Christine sing directly into the Angel of the Lord's mike to bolster the multitude of heavenly host. I told Christine to stand next to Mason (the Angel of the Lord) and take over after he had announced, "Fear not, I bring you glad tidings of great joy!" However, I forgot to tell Mason.

As head angel, first-grader Mason was not going to allow kindergartener Christine any time on his mike. Mason rubbed the feathers off Christine's furry white wings as he bumped her away, and crowded his haloed head into *his* mike. Wings flapped, and the angel chorus nearly took flight. "Gloria! Gloria!" the other angels sang as two microphoned angels fought hard over their *own* glory.

I continued conducting the song from below, my flailing arms imitating the angelic ones above. What else could I do? Christine was doing exactly what she was supposed to do; and my Angel of the Lord had been taught that choir members should never sing directly into the mike unless performing a solo—especially not the *Angel of the Lord's* mike. The audience howled with laughter as they watched the battle in the heavenly places. For many, it was the highlight of that year's Christmas pageant.

What will *your* highlight be this year? It probably won't be something perfectly planned. Let's face it, Christmas will not be perfect. Thank goodness! Imperfection helps us remember to focus on the perfection of the One having the birthday.

This is the second day of a month of watching the world celebrate the *holidays.* Can you return it to the *"holy" days?* Watch for Jesus in small and large events. Nothing will be perfect except the child in the manger. Keep your eyes on Him, and you will not be disappointed.

Response: *Father, Help me to trust in You, for You are my rock eternal. Keep my mind stayed on you throughout this amazing month. May I experience your peace among the busyness. Help me see humor and joy and learn through imperfection. Let me be surprised by all You have to teach me as I fix my eyes on Your perfect Son.*

December 3—Decorating from the Inside Out

Light: *Therefore, as God's chosen people, holy and dearly loved, clothe yourselves with compassion, kindness, humility, gentleness and patience. Bear with each other and forgive whatever grievances you may have against one another. Forgive as the Lord forgave you. And over all these virtues put on love, which binds them all together in perfect unity* (Colossians 3:12–14).

Reflection:

One Christmas, my sister-in-law hauled out all her Christmas decorations and went about her house making merry. When she finished decorating, she stood back and declared in disgust, "It looks like someone just threw up Christmas." Not a very pleasant description, but perhaps somewhat fitting of the glitz, glamour, and tinsel of our holiday décor. She promptly did some undecorating and donated her excess to friends.

One evening I came home after my husband and daughters had strung the Christmas tree lights. They had left the tree lights on, and I could see what appeared to be a signal light blinking for me to turn left at the doorway to the family room. Flashing from the top of the tree was a plastic angel. I felt as if I were in the super shopper lane at a mega mall. That year we rarely turned on the tree lights; they were distracting.

What else distracts us from experiencing a Christmas full of peace and love? As women, we bring warmth into our homes. If our homes look great from the outside, but lack warmth and the visible reminder of God's love, then our houses are merely noisy gongs, or badly blinking lights where Christmas was just "thrown up."

What's inside? Love, joy, and peace? Do we encourage one another with kind and loving words? Do we *consider it all joy* no matter the difficulties of December? Do we enjoy peaceful December evenings, or do we play divide and conquer as our activities scatter family members all over town?

If the exteriors of our houses are decorated, but the interiors are not properly dressed, we can't call these structures homes. Love is more important than perfect lights, decorated cookies, and the tallest spruce in the front window. This Christmas give yourself permission to simplify with a nativity set and a few votive candles. Simplification may add more peaceful quality time and help you celebrate the heart and soul of Christmas.

> If the exteriors of our houses are decorated, but the interiors are not properly dressed, we can't call these structures homes.

Response: *My Creator, fill my heart with compassion, love, and joy. As I decorate my home, let me decorate it with love. May each decoration point to the perfect gift of Your Son. Help me remember that the outside is not what counts and that simplicity might help me better focus on You.*

December 4—Sharing the Good News

Light: *In him was life, and that life was the light of men. The light shines in the darkness, but the darkness has not understood it* (John 1:4–5).

Reflection:

I was in a restaurant where the waitress admitted with embarrassment, "We're not allowed to say, 'Merry Christmas.'" Perhaps the waitress can't say, "Merry Christmas," but I sure can! MERRY CHRISTMAS! JESUS IS BORN! Not only can we say "Merry Christmas," we can say much, much more. We're not mute like Zechariah!

One December, my nephew Jeff's teacher encouraged parents to share their holiday traditions with the second grade class. My sister-in-law Caroline volunteered to explain how our extended family dramatizes the nativity each Christmas Eve. The teacher was cautious because she only wanted secular traditions. But Caroline explained she couldn't go in and just talk about Santa because her son would be completely confused by this unfamiliar depiction of their family celebration.

The teacher reluctantly agreed to allow Caroline to share if she left out the angel and religious words such as "miracle," "glory," "praise," and "God." Caroline brought a nativity set and several costumes and explained our family tradition of having each of the eight cousins dress as a nativity character and act out the Christmas story. A new baby in the family always played baby Jesus, and some little ones were costumed as sheep or a star. She framed the simple story as a birthday party.

"Christmas is about a birthday party—Jesus' birthday," she began. "When Jesus was born, many guests came to His party," she continued. "Joseph was there, and Jesus' mother, Mary, was there." Then Caroline's younger daughter blurted out, "But Joseph isn't Jesus' Daddy!" Caroline thought she'd never be asked back again.

"Joseph is Mary's husband," she continued as she pulled out an assortment of costumes. "He was there, too," she added as she held up a shepherd's cloak and a Magi's crown. "The shepherds left their sheep and came to the birthday party, and wise men came bringing gifts." The children watched in wonder, fascinated with a birthday party so dissimilar to their own.

"Jeffrey played Baby Jesus in our church Christmas pageant when he was two months old!" All eyes turned toward Jeff who couldn't decide if he was proud or slightly embarrassed. "He was a quiet Baby Jesus until the organ played 'Silent Night,' and scared him so badly he began screaming." The children laughed, and Jeff nodded as if he remembered the event.

Caroline bore witness that Christmas is a celebration of Jesus' birth and exposed some children to their first experience with the Christ child.

You bring a special perspective to the re-telling of this story. Who is Jesus to you today? Is He merely a baby in a manger, or the King of your life? Be prepared to make a defense for the One whose birthday you celebrate in December.

Today ask God to show you someone who needs to hear the story and ask God for the sensitivity and wisdom to tell it. Maybe your listener will never hear the words of Matthew, Mark, Luke, or John, but they will hear the gospel through you.

> Who is Jesus to you today? Be prepared to make a defense for the One whose birthday you celebrate in December.

Response: *Dear Lord, I have a story to tell. Prepare me to share it with others. Show me who needs to hear about how you came to earth and prepare their hearts to hear the message.*

December 5—Time for Pondering

Light: *"Be still, and know that I am God; I will be exalted among the nations, I will be exalted in the earth"* (Psalm 46:10).

Reflection:

By December 5th, most of the days on the December calendar are filled. There's the church Christmas pageant, the school winter music program, the office holiday party, your daughter's basketball games, a neighborhood dinner, and family gatherings. Between all this, you'll decorate your home, bake cookies, and buy and wrap gifts. That's the holiday timetable.

Consider Mary's schedule. Within a few months she was visited by an angel, was overcome by the Holy Spirit, learned she was pregnant with the Son of God, broke up and reunited with her betrothed, took a lengthy trip, returned, and traveled to a foreign village while nine months pregnant. Not only that, she gave birth in an unfamiliar place and was inundated by unknown visitors. That is a lot of Life Change Units or LCU's.

LCU's were studied by Doctors Thomas Holmes and Richard Rahe in 1967 as a part of their Social Readjust-

Rating Scale (SRRS). Their testing revealed stressful events have a direct correlation with illness. Included in the list were some of the following good and bad stressors: marital separation, marriage, reconciliation with spouse, pregnancy, major change in financial state, changing to a different line of work, change in living conditions, change in residence, change in number of family gatherings, and even Christmas![1] Looking at Mary's changes, she had a score of over three hundred within twelve months, thus an eighty percent chance of increased illness.

And yet, instead of fretting, she was left pondering. We never hear her holler, "I'm too stressed out! Will all you shepherds take your smelly sheep out of here and give a lady some rest? Joseph, is this cave really the only place in town? If those magi are so wise, why did they bring the baby incense? We've GOTTA get this kid some clothes! Can somebody send for my MOTHER?" Instead, the Bible just says she pondered all these things in her heart. What was it that made her heart so capable of handling this pressure?

> Instead of fretting, Mary was left "pondering." What was it that made her heart so capable of handling this pressure?

I wonder if her heart was a bit like a filing cabinet filled with scripture. She knew she was living out Old Testament prophecy she had studied. She understood she was a part of a wonderful promise as God gave her multiple confirmations of His presence.

It wasn't a stress-free Christmas, but the Prince of Peace was there. It was all she needed, and He's still all we need for these holidays. Let's prepare our hearts with prayer and study so that despite the Life Change Units of the holidays, we treasure and ponder the wonder of our Savior.

Response: *My Rock and My Refuge, I want to be still. I want to sit in Your presence and treasure Immanuel. You are my Prince of Peace. You are all I need. No matter what changes around me, You are constant. In a busy and hectic world, I need to be quiet and know that You are Sovereign and You are in control. Fill my heart with your peace.*

December 6—Daddy, Daddy!

Light: *But when the time had fully come, God sent his Son, born of a woman, born under law, to redeem those under law, that we might receive the full rights of sons. Because you are sons,*

God sent the Spirit of his Son into our hearts, the Spirit who calls out, "Abba, Father" (Galatians 4:4–6).

Yet to all who received him, to those who believed in his name, he gave the right to become children of God—children born not of natural descent, nor of human decision or a husband's will, but born of God (John 1:12–13).

Reflection:

My friend Janet and family began a twenty-four-hour journey to Russia just before Christmas to adopt a six-month old baby girl they named Sarah. What a Christmas present for them, and what a change for Sarah! Instead of living as an orphan, she was welcomed into a wonderful family of four living on seven acres in the country.

Soon after Jeff and Jill adopted a baby boy, they received a call from their international adoption agency telling them, "Your little girl from China is ready!" Their papers were "mistakenly" not put on hold. After looking at the little girl's file, they were off to China in the middle of a typhoon to adopt Lydia, an eighteen-month-old with the same birth date as her six-month-old baby brother. There was no "mistake"—Lydia belongs in their family.

My friend Barbara and her husband Tripp's eighth child was born with Down Syndrome. He so increased their heart and love capacity they adopted three more boys with Down Syndrome. All of these children were chosen, loved, named, and adopted. There's nothing better than an adoption story with a happy ending!

The genealogy of Christ is full of births and adoptions, full of interesting individuals grafted into the faith. Mary's husband, Joseph is an adopted "dad." And when we believe in Jesus, we, too, are adopted children of God, heirs through Christ (see Romans 8:16–17).

> *The Spirit himself testifies with our spirit that we are God's children. Now if we are children, then we are heirs—heirs of God and co-heirs with Christ (Romans 8:16–17).*

Who wouldn't want to cry out "Daddy! Daddy!" and run into the arms of a loving God who longs to nurture and give His children good things? How wonderful to be the apple of God's eye or nestle under the shadow of His wing. And what father doesn't delight in hearing, "Daddy! Daddy!" as his child runs for a warm embrace? God must love to hear us call!

Like the children from the stories, when we are adopted, we experience change. We are loved, chosen, and given the name "Child of God." We retain that title for eternity. Embrace that today as you go about your "Christmasing." Indeed, it is a merry thought!

Response: *Abba Father, thank you for adopting me and being my Daddy. Let me run into your arms each day. Keep me as the apple of Your eye, hide me in the shadow of Your wing. I love to be called Your child.*

December 7—Truth among the Trimmings

Light: *He is the image of the invisible God, the firstborn over all creation. For by him all things were created: things in heaven and on earth, visible and invisible, whether thrones or powers or rulers or authorities; all things were created by him and for him. He is before all things, and in him all things hold together. And he is the head of the body, the church; he is the beginning and the firstborn from among the dead, so that in everything he might have the supremacy. For God was pleased to have all his fullness dwell in him, and through him to reconcile to himself all things, whether things on earth or things in heaven, by making peace through his blood, shed on the cross* (Colossians 1:15–20).

Suggestion: Understanding the Meaning behind Our Decorations

Some claim most of our decorations, traditions, and celebrations have pagan roots. They are partly correct. Christians did reinterpret many of the symbols of their pagan neighbors over the centuries: mistletoe, candles, holly and ivy, the Christmas tree, and caroling. Even gift giving has pagan roots.

Some are troubled by the term "Xmas," assuming it's a shortened, commercialized, and secular way to spell Jesus' birthday. But originally this term had religious significance. X is the Greek letter *Chi*, and many centuries ago scribes, monks, and theologians used it as a symbol for Xristos or *Christos*—the Greek equivalent of "Christ." The symbol X was often drawn at the place where a believer sacrificed his life for Christ. What a remarkable reminder of faith

> Some claim most of our decorations, traditions, and celebrations have pagan roots. They are partly correct.

and devotion. The X is also an example of how understanding the symbols and their meanings encourages our celebration of Xmas.[2]

Even the date of December 25th may have been a knockoff of pagan tradition. December 25th was the birthday of Sol Invictus, the unconquered sun god. Greeks partied at the return of the sun. Similarly, Romans celebrated Saturnalia, their winter solstice festival, from December 17th through December 24th with great merrymaking, gambling, and gift giving. In the 4th century the church put Christ's birthday on the pagan god's birthday, in effect stealing or co-opting the holiday. Does this trouble me? Not at all. The "birth" of the "sun god" deities pales in comparison to the birth of the Son of God.[3]

He is the One who created the sun and the One who will never be conquered. He is the Alpha and Omega, the Beginning and the End. He is the firstborn of all creation. On December 25th we don't celebrate the return of sunshine; we celebrate the coming of the Son! And instead of Saturn, the god of peace and plenty, we worship the true Prince of Peace!

Knowing the exact date Christ was born is less important than knowing about His birth, how He lived and died, and rose again. The most significant date to know is the day He was born in our hearts.

We're also not sure which *year* He was born. But in AD 525 it was set (though incorrectly) after Pope John the first asked Dionysius Exiguus (Dionysius the Small) a Roman monk, mathematician, and astronomer to create a standardized calendar.[4] Dionysius labeled Jesus' birth during the year AD 1. Unfortunately, the year coincided with the reign of a persecutor of the faith, so the date was altered. It is now believed Jesus was born *Before Christ* (BC).[5] Confusing? Oh, a little! Historical records and the annals of Josephus lead us to believe that Herod died around 4 BC, so we know Jesus was not born in AD 1 because the Magi visited Herod in a very living way! Thus, Jesus' date of birth is now estimated to be around 4 or 5 BC.[6]

We have all these questions: *when* (day and year) was He born, *where* was He born, in *what* was He born, *how* was He born? But the most important question is *why*.

> Knowing the exact date Christ was born is less important than knowing about His birth, how He lived and died, and rose again.

This is easily answered in 1 John 4:10 —"This is love: not that we loved God, but that he loved us and sent his Son as an atoning sacrifice for our sins."

This year, when you decorate, try to learn what the symbols mean in a Christian context and be prepared to share the true and original meaning with others. It's an intriguing conversation starter!

> This year, when you decorate, try to learn what the symbols mean in a Christian context and be prepared to share the Christian symbolism with others.

Symbol: The Holly and the Ivy

It would be wonderful if every symbol such as Xmas were another way of looking at Christ or could be transformed into that. For example, holly, though rooted in pagan superstitions, has no power beyond its beauty. However, it is a powerful visual reminder for Christians.

Originally, holly and ivy decorated altars, temples, and sanctuaries. The early church members often had to decorate with pagan symbols such as holly (though they didn't believe in its magical powers) in order to save themselves from recognition and thus persecution.[7]

But like so many of the other pagan traditions, Christian leaders usurped the decoration and turned it into a Christian symbol. Pope Gregory the Great claimed that it was fine to have holly and ivy decorating churches. After all, why not have the gifts of nature bring tribute to Christ?[8]

Each Christmas season, the holly's sharp points remind us of the crown of thorns; the green leaves represent eternal life; the red berries point us to the blood of Christ; and the bitter green bark reminds us of the cross.[9]

Like many Christmas carols, "The Holly and the Ivy" speaks more to Easter than Christ's birth.

Song: "The Holly and the Ivy"
The holly bears a blossom,
As white as lily flow'r,
And Mary bore sweet Jesus Christ,
To be our dear Savior
The holly bears a berry,
As red as any blood,
And Mary bore sweet Jesus Christ,
To do poor sinners good.

The holly bears a prickle,
As sharp as any thorn,
And Mary bore sweet Jesus Christ,
On Christmas Day in the morn
The holly bears a bark,
As bitter as the gall,
And Mary bore sweet Jesus Christ,
For to redeem us all

The verses all close with reminding us, *"And Mary bore sweet Jesus Christ"*—that part is Christmas, but the reasons are Easter:

> *To be our dear Savior,*
> *To do poor sinners good,*
> *For to redeem us all*

There is no way to celebrate His birth without knowing of His death and understanding His resurrection. Follow the star to the cross!

Christ is born! Gloria!

Christ died for you and rose again! Alleluia!

December 8—Christmas Cards

Light: *For God, who said, "Let light shine out of darkness," made his light shine in our hearts to give us the light of the knowledge of the glory of God in the face of Christ. But we have this treasure in jars of clay to show that this all-surpassing power is from God and not from us* (2 Corinthians 4:6–7).

Reflection:

I love Christmas cards. During the month of December, I look forward to opening the mailbox and finding real mail. "Snail-mail," with my name and address handwritten across the front, represents an opportunity to catch up with old friends and family through photos and letters, sharing highlights from their year.

The mail is usually positive. Most Christmas cards celebrate successes and omit difficulties. When we write of the year's highlights, we don't include marital problems or discipline problems with our children, and we usually spare our readers the details about caring for our elderly parents. Such unattractive details are almost more than we can handle, so why would we want others to know them? But maybe it would be a relief to our readers if we could be more vulnerable. We should consider the genealogy of Jesus before we inject our positive spin into our Christmas card yearly updates. You may remember our November study where we focused on some of the "black sheep" and bad decisions among those in Jesus' ancestral heritage.

> We should consider the genealogy of Jesus before we inject positive spin into our Christmas card yearly updates.

The Bible isn't afraid to reveal the mistakes of its main characters, so why should we be so timid in revealing our flaws? Rahab is labeled a harlot and yet because she trusted in God rather than men, Rahab is one of two women listed in Hebrews 11, the Bible's "Hall of Faith" chapter. The lowlights are revealed because God is in the middle of both lowlights and highlights and can turn both into His glory.

I recently went to a friend's funeral. Her husband described his fifteen-year marriage as the "best eight years of his life." He was vulnerable and honest about the rough first seven years, but also shared that after they worked on their marriage, they became best friends.

Sadly, the last three years were spent enduring the ravages of cancer. Their commitment was such a testimony. Knowing their marriage wasn't always perfect helped all of us see the benefits of working through our own difficulties, with God's help. Perfection is hard to relate to. But weakness, made strong in Christ, is not only encouraging, but also empowering.

Maybe this year was difficult for you. Maybe you're not sure your Christmas card and letter measure up. It doesn't matter. You measure up in God's eyes. And whatever problems threaten to bind you are nothing for the One who was not bound by death. Give your troubles to your heavenly Father and He'll help you work through them. He is Immanuel— God with you.

Response: *Heavenly Father, You know my struggles. May your all-surpassing power be my strength. Let me glorify You in my weakness as Your light shines through me.*

December 9—We Have a Redeemer!

Light: *"For I know the plans I have for you," declares the LORD, "plans to prosper you and not to harm you, plans to give you hope and a future"* (Jeremiah 29:11).

Reflection:

One cold December evening after performing, "O Holy Night," I drove home recalling its lines, "He knows our needs, to our weakness is no stranger." I was lonely and tired, and I really questioned their truth. I felt God had forgotten my needs and ignored my prayers.

Have you ever felt that way? Perhaps you've never received the deserved promotion. Or perhaps you've lost a husband, are childless, or feel lonely.

Ruth was homeless, childless, and husbandless. I wonder how she felt? But look at her. Ruth, a Moabitess, seemingly had more faith in Naomi's God than Naomi did because of something she saw, knew, or felt about God.

God had not forgotten these two women. He had a wonderful future planned for both, and it wasn't just leftovers. When Ruth harvested in Boaz's fields, she might have thought she was gleaning—merely picking up forgotten and unwanted leftovers from the ground. But Boaz had deliberately left plenty of good grain. Similarly, we may think we're gleaning leftovers, but God is throwing much more our way than we can imagine. It's time to look for it!

Ruth's obedience, love, and dedication led her to her redeemer. She found a wonderfully dear and protective man who would father a child in the line of David and ultimately in the line of Christ.

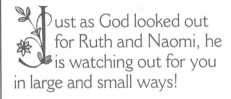

Just as God looked out for Ruth and Naomi, he is watching out for you in large and small ways!

Consider Naomi. She felt hopeless, certain she'd never have another child, let alone a descendant. And yet, Naomi moved back in the direction where her faith could be rekindled. She returned to Bethlehem where she discovered God was watching out for her.

God is watching out for you in large and small ways, too. He takes your past hurts, and then works to heal and redeem them. You are not forgotten. God knows exactly where you are, what you need, and whom—through trials and testing—you are becoming. Keep gleaning. God has a hope and a future for you.

Response: *Heavenly Father, even when I don't know my future, I know You have a plan. Help me to seek Your will and Your ways today and always. I know You are a good Father who wants me to grow to know You more. Help me to trust in the hope and future you have planned for me in Christ.*

December 10—Forgiving Scrooge

Light: *"Come now, let us reason together," says the* LORD, *"Though your sins are like scarlet, they shall be as white as snow; though they are red as crimson, they shall be like wool"* (Isaiah 1:18).

As far as the east is from the west, so far has he removed our transgressions from us (Psalms 103:12).

Reflection:

While watching *A Christmas Carol* I was struck by Scrooge's ability to forgive himself and get on with life. He saw his past mistakes, his present mistakes, recognized where they were leading, and made a change.

Crazy old Ebenezer Scrooge encouraged me. He wasted not a minute of grief over his past. Instead of wallowing in guilt over his cruelty, regretting where his choices had taken him, and feeling depressed over age and circumstances, he chose joy. He determined to spend the rest of his days doing good, generously bestowing his love, finances, and attention upon all those he met.

In a funny way, Scrooge reminds me of David. David could have beaten himself up over his past sins, of which there were many. Instead, David worshiped the Lord and got on with His life, knowing He had been forgiven.

> Crazy old Ebenezer Scrooge encouraged me. He wasted not a minute of grief over his past and determined to spend the rest of his days doing good.

Can we allow ourselves to experience that kind of grace? We need to. God wants us to get on with our lives. Once we've asked for forgiveness and repented, God forgives us and describes us as *white as snow*. To God we look blindingly beautiful in our purity. We can pick ourselves up and praise God, like David, or run out and bring good cheer like Ebenezer.

When someone asks "Are you in the Christmas spirit?" remember that through God's gifts of grace and forgiveness, we can experience the joyous wonder of giving and loving others. Now that's Christmas spirit!

Response: *Gracious Father, Sometimes I feel so guilty about the choices I've made. I confess and ask your forgiveness. Help me to accept your forgiveness, and to forgive myself so I can serve you with freedom and joy this Christmas.*

December 11—The Fragrance of Christ

Light: *But thanks be to God, who always leads us in triumphal procession in Christ and through us spreads everywhere the fragrance of the knowledge of him. For we are to God the aroma of Christ among those who are being saved and those who are perishing* (2 Corinthians 2:14–15).

Reflection:

One of my favorite parts of Christmas is hearing music everywhere I go from Thanksgiving to New Year's. Each carol holds memories, making me reminisce about the past and focus my heart on Jesus. I hope this season you hear the music of Christmas in a new way, understanding how the scriptures reveal the prophecy of His coming, the revelation of His birth, His death, and His second coming.

"Lo How a Rose" reminds me of what we've learned in Isaiah. Remember the tender shoot? Jesus, the rose, bloomed in Bethlehem so long ago and continues to bloom in the hearts of those who receive Him. The carol reminds us that Jesus is a stem from Jesse's lineage.

> *Lo how a rose e'er blooming,*
> *From tender stem hath sprung,*
> *Of Jesse's lineage coming,*
> *As saints of old have sung.*
> *It came, a flower bright, amid the cold of winter,*
> *When half-spent was the night.*
> *Isaiah 'twas foretold it,*
> *The Rose I have in mind,*
> *With Mary we behold it,*
> *The virgin mother kind.*
> *To show God's love aright,*

She bore to us a Savior,
When half spent was the night.

A subsequent verse tells about the fragrance and the light of Christ, and that Jesus is fully man and fully God. Like so many of our carols, this verse points toward our future with Christ. What a marvelous thought! Today, let's be the fragrance of Christ and a light wherever we go, carrying with us the thought that one day we'll convene in the bright courts of heaven for a day that will never end.

Response: *Holy Father, Help me be Your fragrance and Your light to others. May the joy of experiencing Your presence radiate from me. Thank You for being the New Testament fulfillment of Old Testament promises. May I walk in the knowledge that I have an eternity to grow in You.*

December 12—The Obedience of Joseph

Light: *Your word is a lamp to my feet and a light for my path* (Psalm 119:105).

I have hidden your word in my heart that I might not sin against you (Psalm 119:11).

Reflection:

Recently I read a fabulous book on parenting. The only problem is that when my kids disobey, I always forget its great solutions. I really need to review that book more often. I need its practical wisdom fresh on my mind at the beginning of the day, and I need to reflect on it as I prepare to go to sleep.

The Bible is like that, too, but even more so. I need it fresh on my mind for the immediacy of the day as well as to build a foundation for the future. And I need it as I go to bed so I can meditate on its wisdom.

Someone once pointed out that there are thirty-one chapters in Proverbs, one to read for each day of the month. I wonder how I'd respond on a daily basis if wise proverbs were fresh on my mind? Would it help me be more obedient to God?

Joseph was obedient to God and followed directions without question. He was constantly told what to do, where to go, and when to leave. His obedience seemed so natural. We never hear Him say, "But God, that instruction seems a little strange. Did you say *Egypt?* The people of our faith don't live *there*!" His obedience resulted in salvation instead of death at the hands of Herod's soldiers.

So often we're unsure what to do, yet we have a book full of instructions. Maybe we need to place it near our beds so we'll study God's wise advice in the morning, and reflect on His teaching before we sleep, always ready to learn with a willing heart. The Holy Spirit instructs us by day and by night. Imagine what we could learn if we let Him speak to us through His Word on a daily basis. The best Christmas book we have is the most authoritative book ever written about Christ—the Bible. Now is a great time to make a habit of reading it!

> The best Christmas book we have is the most authoritative book ever written about Christ—the Bible. Now is a great time to make a habit of reading it!

Response: *O God, I will open Your Word today and tomorrow. May I find joy as I immerse myself in Your teaching. Prepare my heart to understand what I read. I need to spend time with You each day so Your words are fresh, treasured, stored, and filed for easy access. May these words be a lamp and a light today as I walk with You.*

December 13—Step Right Up to God in Prayer

Light: *In the morning, O LORD, you hear my voice; in the morning I lay my requests before you and wait in expectation* (Psalm 5:3).

By day the LORD directs his love, at night his song is with me—a prayer to the God of my life (Psalm 42:8).

Reflection:

Do you see the theme in today's scriptures? They remind us that all day long we can boldly come before our God. And yet we take this privilege for granted. Before Christ's resurrection, when a priest approached God, it was nothing like what we now experience in coming before Him.

If you've ever tried to read through the Bible in a year, some of the details in the construction of the temple may have kept you from completing your goal. The tabernacle was a holy place, built exactly the way God commanded (see Exodus 40:1–8 and

Hebrews 9:1–14). You may have wondered, "Why on earth do I need to read specifics about the dimensions, veils, colors, jewels on the breastplate, and the amount of flour in each loaf of bread?" There is a reason. Keep plugging on.

In the holy place rested an altar of incense, a lampstand, a table for the shewbread. Walled off by a thick veil, which horses could not pull apart, was the holiest of holies. This housed the Ark of covenant box containing the Ten Commandments, manna, and Aaron's Rod.[10] But all that is history. When Christ rose, that four-inch thick veil split from the top to the bottom so that now, through faith in Him, we can come before God with bold confidence.

Therefore, brothers, since we have confidence to enter the Most Holy Place by the blood of Jesus, by a new and living way opened for us through the curtain, that is, his body, and since we have a great priest over the house of God, let us draw near to God with a sincere heart in full assurance of faith, having our hearts sprinkled to cleanse us from a guilty conscience and having our bodies washed with pure water. Let us hold unswervingly to the hope we profess, for he who promised is faithful (Hebrews 10:19–23).

Jesus Christ replaced the old with the new. In revealing the Old Testament details, we see how Christ is the New Testament fulfilled. Christ is our High Priest and He is the Sacrifice. He is the Bread of the Presence. He is Mercy. He is the Lampstand, the Altar of Incense, the Veil, and the Tabernacle.[11]

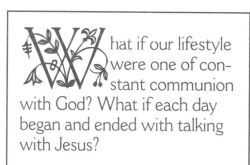

What if our lifestyle were one of constant communion with God? What if each day began and ended with talking with Jesus?

Now we can come directly to God in prayer, anytime, anyplace. What a privilege! What if our lifestyle were one of constant communion with God? What if each day began and ended with talking with Jesus? What are we missing by not using our personal prayer hotline to God? Maybe this next year can be a year of talking to Him with a sincere heart and the full assurance of faith that He sees, hears, and loves us.

Response: *Dear God, I come before you with confidence through Jesus Christ. Thank you for Your forgiveness. I draw near to you with a sincere heart and the full assurance of your saving grace. Lord, jog my memory to pray all day so we're in constant fellowship.*

December 14—Rejoice, Rejoice!

Light: *Rejoice in the Lord always. I will say it again: Rejoice!*
(Philippians 4:4).

Reflection:

Heinrich Seuse (Suso), although a German born into wealth, became a Dominican monk who shared the gospel with common people. Unfortunately, he was condemned, exiled, and persecuted for his radical beliefs that the gospel was for all.

In a dream, he saw angels singing and dancing with joy and woke up to write, "In Dulci Jubilo!" in German and Latin." This mixed-language (macaronic) carol is most definitely not a solemn scriptural song in the high language of the 14th century, but instead an exuberant song for all classes celebrating the joy of believing.

Hundreds of years later, James Mason Neale, a man also persecuted and exiled for the radical belief that the joy of Christianity was for all people, translated this happy carol into English "Good Christian Men, Rejoice!" so many could rejoice.

Picture caroling in merry old England, with string and wind instruments—even a bass fiddle—encircling torch-bearing carolers. They're celebrating great news. Jesus Christ was *born to save!* Is that invitation enough to celebrate? Suso and Neale thought so. Rejoice today! Again, I say rejoice!

Song: "Good Christian Men, Rejoice!"

Good Christian men, rejoice with heart and soul and voice;
Give ye heed to what we say: News! News! Jesus Christ is born today:
Ox and ass before him bow and He is in the manger now
Christ is born today! Christ is born today!

Good Christian men, rejoice with heart and soul and voice;
Now ye hear of endless bliss; Joy! Joy! Jesus Christ was born for this!
He has open'd the heav'nly door and man is blessed evermore
Christ was born for this! Christ was born for this!

Good Christian men, rejoice with heart and soul and voice;
Now ye need not fear the grave; Peace! Peace! Jesus Christ was born to save!
Calls you one and calls you all to gain his everlasting hall
Christ was born to save! Christ was born to save!

Symbol: Light

Christmas lights outline rooftops and windows, encircle evergreens and illuminate front yards in our town. I especially enjoy seeing single candle lights twinkling in windows to welcome me home. How appropriate that we celebrate with light on the birthday of the One who is the One true light.

In ancient times, unbelievers lit winter bonfires as a plea to the sun to remain during the darkness.[12] They considered the lighting of candles to hold great power, yet remained in darkness to the One True Light, the real Son with whom resides all power.

When the candles flicker in your home, consider their symbolism. The people of old sat in darkness waiting for their Savior. Zechariah tells us God sent His Son "to shine on those living in darkness and in the shadow of death, to guide our feet into the path of peace" (Luke 1:79).

Let Him illuminate your path of peace this Advent season. Here are a few suggestions to keep remembering His light.

Suggestion: Jesus Is the Light

One year I received tin luminaries from a student and his parents. They drilled holes into tin cans, placed a candle inside and included the verse, "Jesus is the Light of the World!" Another year, my daughters painted a simple design on clear, glass votive candleholders and gave them as gifts. Perhaps this year, with candles and luminaries, you could bring the gift of light into the lives of your friends, and with an added scripture, the light of Christ.

Let the light of Christ shine through you like luminaries lining the porch steps to your home. Draw others to the One who calls Himself "The Door" of salvation.

Response: *Light of the World, shine Your light through me. May those who do not know You see the light of Your Son's face in me. As I go through my day, guide me by Your all-surpassing power.*

December 15—A Powerful Answer to Prayer

Light: *Do not be anxious about anything, but in everything, by prayer and petition, with thanksgiving, present your requests to God. And the peace of God, which transcends all understanding, will guard your hearts and your minds in Christ Jesus (Philippians 4:6–7).*

Reflection:

Do you have a Zechariah prayer? Is there something you've longed for, prayed about, and then questioned God's timing? Do you believe God is hearing you? No doubt Zechariah, an old man, yet to be called into the holy temple, might have felt like that. But he was faithful, and he remained righteous.

Maybe you've been faithful, but your "nothing is impossible with God" prayer remains unanswered. But in one momentous encounter, God answered Zechariah's prayers of the past, present, plus the prayers of thousands of Jews for many centuries.

God's answers and ways are not always our ways (Romans 11:33–34). God's timing is not always our timing. Can you imagine how God might have longed to give Zechariah and Elizabeth the whole picture during the decades they prayed for a child? "Zechariah, you *will* have a child, and he won't just be *any* child. He will prepare the way for the Messiah!" What glorious news that *would* have been for a younger Zechariah! What glorious news it *should* have been for an older Zechariah. Instead, Zechariah said he needed a sign.

Sometimes God says "Yes"; sometimes, "No"; and sometimes, "Wait." Why he finally answered Zechariah' prayers with a "Yes, I heard you," and does not answer all the prayers of the righteous with a "Yes," I do not know.

I have an aunt with treatable, but incurable lymphoma. Why God doesn't make it treatable and *curable*, I do not know. But she remains faithful in thanksgiving and praise, and she is an example to many of the benefits of being a prayer warrior.

We can look to Zechariah and have great hope. The Lord heard Zechariah. He hears us as well!

We can look to Zechariah and have great hope. God has a plan. The Lord heard Zechariah. He hears you. Ask Him for what you need. Do not become discouraged. Stay near to Him. Be faithful in prayer. He loves you.

Response: *Omniscient Father, You know what I've been bringing to you over and over and over. As I pray today, I understand You know what's best for me. You see the bigger picture, and you know the proper timing. Help me be faithful and righteous as I wait on Your plan and Your answer. Amen.*

December 16th—Zechariah's Song of Prophecy and Praise

Light: *"The LORD your God is with you, he is mighty to save. He will take great delight in you, he will quiet you with his love, he will rejoice over you with singing"* (Zephaniah 3:17).

Reflection:

My speech therapist ordered me to go on vocal rest for a month from December 10 through January 7. "Impossible!" I told her. "I have to direct four Christmas pageants this week, and I'm going home for the holidays to catch up with friends and family!" She responded by writing me a list: no talking, no coughing, no laughing. She might as well have put me in a dark room with white noise. For me, the holidays were over.

That Christmas I held a sign in front of me: ZECHARI-AH. It always got a laugh. But during that December, I began to understand his pain. Communication was slow and clunky with hand motions and hastily scribbled notes. And when I would talk with my hands or silently mouth my words, my friends would imitate me, forgetting they could talk.

My husband became the interpreter, and I became the listener, a frustrating identity change. I never realized how much I used my voice until I tried to direct a show, corral my kids, or greet friends at a Christmas gathering. Although my damaged vocal cords still worked, each day of silence meant healing and a day closer to being able to sing God's praises with a reliable voice.

Zechariah had it a lot worse. He couldn't talk for nine months, which must have reduced his capacity to serve as a priest. He must have been frustrated. I wonder what his silence taught him.

My husband considered my prescribed silence as a gift. No, it is not because I talk too much! His reasons for thinking this way became clear to me as well. The inability to speak made me a better, more sensitive listener. Quiet people were suddenly comfortable around a less outgoing me. In addition to listening, I really *heard* what people said. Speaking through writing or motions, I discovered I had a curious and captive audience. In conversation, less was more!

This is a season to listen. We hear brass music and Christmas carols; we listen to bells ringing, and we cherish the sound of children's laughter. We also need to listen to God, friends, husband, and children. Try asking questions and waiting long enough for your loved ones to expand their answers. Don't join in every discussion or song. Instead meditate on what you hear. The sounds of the season are a gift, opened with your ears. Are you quiet enough to hear God singing over you? Listen and learn what the Lord of Love has to say to you today.

> Christmas is a season to listen. We need to listen to the carols and cherish the sound of our children's laughter. Most importantly, we need to listen to God.

Response: *Divine Composer, open my ears that I may hear Your music all around me. Thank You for singing and exulting over me with shouts of joy. Quiet my lips so I listen more than speak. Help me hear Your voice and understand Your words.*

December 17—Nothing Is Impossible with God!

Light: *"My grace is sufficient for you, for my power is made perfect in weakness." Therefore I will boast all the more gladly about my weaknesses, so that Christ's power may rest on me"* (2 Corinthians 12:9).

Reflection:

I'm sure we've all experienced seemingly impossible situations that produce more questions than answers. We can learn from Mary.

When the angel told Mary she would conceive and bear a son and this child would be the long-awaited Messiah, Mary must have been overwhelmed. After all, this was an impossible scenario: Mary had not consummated her relationship with Joseph. Mary's one question "How will this be?" is not of doubt, but of puzzlement. The angel's response is one we should live by daily, for the angel explained, "Nothing is impossible with God." Mary heard the words, believed, and responded with humility, "I am the Lord's servant. May it be to me as you have said."

With God, the impossible becomes possible. An impossible situation becomes a canvas for his creativity and power.

I recently saw an original production of *Little Women*. The stage was small and limited. But the writer/director used this setting to efficiently and intimately tell the story. It seemed the auditorium was built specifically for that production. The structural challenge became the framework for success. Impossible constraints often fuel creativity and inspiration.

Some of the most enduring and creative artistic ventures are borne in times of stress, grief, and exile. In many of the carols we've studied, the composer struggled with a challenge. How many songs could we sing if we allowed God's power to overcome the obstacles? How many problems could be solved with wisdom from above? Life's obstacles provide opportunities for our Creator's power to be revealed. He is a director who knows our limitations and can use them for His glory.

Knowing nothing is impossible with God, what can we look forward to next year? Today, claim, "nothing is impossible with God" in writing or in song. Shout these words aloud

> *Jesus looked at them and said, "With man this is impossible, but with God all things are possible."* (Matthew 19:26) ✵

as you go throughout your day, or post them in big letters on your refrigerator. I don't know what's going on in your life this December, but nothing is impossible with God. You have an everlasting Father! Your journey may be quite different than Mary's; and yet, *nothing is impossible with God.* Not then, and certainly not now.

What are you waiting to do that can be accomplished with His help?

Response: *Dear God, you've given me certain talents. As I look to a new year, I commit these talents to Your glory. Help new songs to be borne in my heart—songs which praise Your awesome power. No obstacle is impossible with You.*

December 18—Being Filled with the Holy Spirit

Light: *But the fruit of the spirit is love, joy, peace, patience, kindness, goodness, faithfulness, gentleness and self-control. Against such things there is no law* (Galatians 5:22–23).

Reflection:

The holidays are filled with the words, "love," "joy," and "peace," and yet, how do we attain these attributes? A dump truck full of these fruits of the spirit will not be unloaded into an unwilling heart. They are gifts from God for the prepared and willing heart of a believer. We can ask for the gifts of love, joy, peace, longsuffering, gentleness, goodness, faith, meekness, and self-control from the Holy Spirit. Isn't it interesting how we pray to *God* for protection and we claim the name of *Jesus*, but we forget to address the *Holy Spirit*? I can tell when I haven't asked for His empowerment because the fruits of the spirit are void in my life.

Though the Holy Spirit was given to us when Christ left the earth, many righteous individuals were filled with the blessing of the Holy Spirit before that. Simeon and Anna recognized the infant as their Savior King. The Holy Spirit was indeed at work in the life of Elizabeth who recognized the miracle in Mary's life. Elizabeth also felt what happened when her unborn son was filled with the Holy Spirit. What a kick (see Luke 1:41)!

When our lives are filled with the Holy Spirit, we perceive things our human eyes cannot fathom. When our lives are filled with the Holy Spirit, energy, joy, and the bubbly effervescence of His love rush out. What are we missing by not including Him in our spiritual lives?

Today, when you pray, acknowledge the Holy Spirit. Ask Him to fill your day with His comfort and presence. Ask Him to help you see Jesus in all you do, to see the needs of others, and to see places to reach out with the fruit of His constant presence. Use your concordance to study love, joy, and peace. Find verses you can claim and live by. Meditate on them, and commit them to memory. The Holy Spirit longs to fill the lives of those who *live by the Spirit* and keep in step with the *Spirit*.

Response: *Lord and Father, fill me with the Presence of Your Holy Spirit. As I read the scriptures, may Your Holy Spirit guide me and offer wisdom. As I pray, may Your Holy Spirit help me utter the words. And as I go through the day, may Your Spirit help me see the world with Your eyes so I might do Your will.*

December 19—Mary's Song

Light: *Because of the LORD's great love we are not consumed, for his compassions never fail. They are new every morning; great is your faithfulness* (Lamentations 3:22–23).

Reflection:

In December of 1929, my German grandmother, Lena Siemens, gave birth to her son Abe in a Moscow hospital. Her second-born son had just died; her husband Nicolai had been arrested for his religious beliefs, and her firstborn son, Little Nick, had been deported hundreds of miles away. She had no clothes or money for her new infant.

Days later, she, along with her temporarily released husband and newborn son, escaped across the Russian border. But she was unable to bring her toddler Little Nick. This was not a perfect Christmas for Lena, Nicolai, or Little Nick. Yet, during a life filled with miraculous God-incidents, she and my grandfather found, and claimed, their life verse: Lamentations 3:22–23.

For my grandparents, the Lord, indeed, was their portion and hope, and they praised Him for His great faithfulness. Two years after their escape, their five-year-old son Nick traveled solo most of the way from the Crimean Peninsula to America to be reunited with his family in McCook, Nebraska.

What is your song? If you don't have your own verse or your own song, ask God to reveal key verses to you. If you have a song, sing it with a full and grateful heart.

It was no surprise that "Great is Thy Faithfulness" was chosen for my grandfather's funeral. This was Nicolai and Lena's song, sung in praise to God for His working in their lives.

What is your song? We don't know what is going to happen in life, but we do know He is faithful and He is Immanuel—God with us. If you don't have your own verse or your own song, ask God to reveal key verses; sing them with a full and grateful heart.

Response: *Lord, each morning I awaken to Your love and compassion. Your love for me is great, and Your compassions never fail. You are my portion and my hope. Reveal new words for me to live by. I want to sing Your praise as I go through my day. I love You, Lord.*

December 20—Songs of Hannah, Zechariah, and Mary

Light: *He was in the world, and though the world was made through him, the world did not recognize him. He came to that which was his own, but his own did not receive him (John 1:10–11).*

Reflection:

One Christmas, we planned to fly from Virginia to Washington State. The night before we left, the temperature dropped, and it began to snow. As I began washing clothes for the trip, I discovered no water could flow into the washing machine because the pipes were frozen. Though I was disheartened at the notion that I could not wash my children's clothes, I struggled more with the thought that the pipes might thaw while we visited in Seattle and we'd return to a flooded house. I decided we couldn't consider flying to Seattle, and Christmas was essentially ruined.

Snow began falling in big, beautiful flakes. My husband took our two-year-old daughter outside to let the snowflakes fall on her face. She delighted in her winter surprise. But my indoor song was one of whining, fear, and grumbling as I crammed packages in suitcases and filled baskets with dirty laundry for my neighbor's machine.

My gracious friend not only washed, but also folded my laundry. We had a change of heart and flew out the next morning. Guess what? The pipes never broke! But I've always been sad I missed my toddler's first taste of snow by refusing to receive the joy of the moment. I did not keep a song in my heart.

Most Bethlehem villagers missed receiving the joy of the moment. Bethlehem was crowded and chaotic. Many never noticed Jesus. Some townsfolk saw only two ragged travelers enter a crowded village. Some may have seen a poor family in a cave. Others saw only a baby in a manger.

Maybe their song was,

> *Taxing taxes by the maxes, for both rich and poor*
> *Senseless census makes us tense, oh bother us no more*
> *Hustle bustle, use your muscle, ain't Herod's plan so grand*
> *As a leader he's a ruler we just cannot stand.*[13]

Jesus was in their midst; yet, did they miss truth and beauty because they were focused on something less wonderful? Were they distracted by the temporary while the eternal God was in their presence?

This Christmas do you recognize and receive Him? Or is your schedule too hectic to let Him in? When you go through a busy city, for whom are you looking? Where could you see

Jesus in the hustle and bustle and lists and lines? He's right there with you.

Why not choose a song this Christmas, one you sing whenever you need to remember that Jesus was there in the midst of Bethlehem's chaos and is there today in the busyness of our lives.

Response: *Dear God, Keep me from focusing on the temporary when Your eternal glory is so much more important. Help me smile when I see examples of Your grace and love throughout the day. May I sing a song of joy that causes others to ask me where it comes from. It comes from You. Let me bring others to the Christ of Christmas.*

December 21—The Twelve Days of Christmas

Symbol, Song, and Suggestion[14]

Today "The Twelve Days of Christmas" is our song, symbol, and even the suggestion! "But why that silly *secular* carol?" you ask. Read on.

Some speculate this song may have been a code used in England in the sixteenth century, a time when Anglican Church teachings were upheld at the expense of all others. Catholic beliefs along with other Protestant beliefs that differed with Anglican teaching were prohibited. According to some, these twelve numbers may have actually taught Catholic children catechisms about the Bible.

Whether or not the allegorical code theory holds any water or is mere conjecture or urban legend, the story still provides a new and amusing way to look at an old song. The correlations are intriguing: the ten lords presiding over the laws of the Ten Commandments, the eight lowly milkmaids no doubt deserving of the blessings of the beatitudes. Look at the days below and the potential tool for helping children memorize biblical facts.

Song and Symbols: "The Twelve Days of Christmas"

My true love	God
Me	the Christian
Partridge in a pear tree	Jesus Christ crucified on a tree. the one protective bird which will sacrifice its life for its young.
Two turtle doves	Old and New Testaments

Three French hens	faith, hope and love (three gifts of the Spirit from 1 Corinthians 13)
	—three expensive French hens: Gold, frankincense and myrrh (Matthew 2:10–11)
Four calling birds	four Gospels that sing the song of salvation through Christ.
Five golden rings	first five books of the Old Testament (Books of Moses)
Six geese a-laying	six days of creation (Genesis 1:1–31)
Seven swans a-swimming	seven spiritual gifts of the Holy Spirit (Romans 12:6–8)
Eight maids a-milking	eight beatitudes (Matthew 5:3–10)
Nine ladies dancing	nine fruits of the Spirit (Galatians 5:22–23)
Ten lords a-leaping	Ten Commandments (Exodus 20:1–17)
Eleven pipers piping	eleven faithful disciples (Acts 1:13; Mark 3:16–19)
Twelve drummers drumming	twelve truths of the Apostles' Creed

Suggestion: The Twelve Days Revisited

The Twelve Days of Christmas begin December 26 and end January 6, the day the church celebrates Epiphany and the arrival of the Magi.

Our family's tradition is to give the *Twelve Days of Christmas* to an unsuspecting friend who needs a little lift. One year we began on the first of December, but another year on December fourteenth with the intention of ending the period on Christmas Day. Choose the most convenient twelve days or maybe even the actual twelve days of Christmas!

> Our family's tradition is to give the "Twelve Days of Christmas to an unsuspecting friend who needs a little lift.

If you're inspired to try this; on the next page is a shopping list of "gifts" to get you started. Make a run to your local craft and dollar stores and you'll be ready to take on the twelve days as a humorous gift idea to brighten someone's Christmas season.

Day One:	Craft store bird stuck on a plastic pear branch
Day Two:	Dove® candy bar and Turtle Candy bar
Day Three:	Rotisserie chicken, French cut green beans, French bread
Day Four:	Dollar store phone with four birds glued onto it, or a phone card
Day Five:	Five glazed donut rings, five party-favor rings, or napkin rings
Day Six:	Six hardboiled eggs decorated with a letter on each spelling *I LOVE U*
Day Seven:	Make salt/flour/water clay swans, or purchase decorative wedding swans
Day Eight:	A carton of eggnog with plastic gloves blown up like udders and attached
Day Nine:	Nine cupcakes with ballerinas or buy one inexpensive doll who writes a note of excuses why the other eight prima donnas couldn't make it
Day Ten:	Ten plastic frogs, or anything that jumps
Day Eleven:	Eleven kazoos or noisemakers
Day Twelve:	A toy drum, a video of you singing the song, or appear at their doorstep to drum a carol

December 22—Giving Thanks

Light: *Be joyful always; pray continually; give thanks in all circumstances, for this is God's will for you in Christ Jesus* (1 Thessalonians 5:16–18).

But thanks be to God! He gives us victory through our Lord Jesus Christ (1 Corinthians 15:57).

Reflection:

Give thanks in everything? You mean even when the sales clerk is rude? Even when no one will smile during the family Christmas card photo shoot? Even when receiving a toaster instead of a toasty cashmere scarf?

One December I prematurely found a gift my husband purchased for me. It wasn't anything I wanted. It was a porcelain egg. Since I don't like knick-knacks, his selection and the waste of money annoyed me. I wasn't looking forward to opening it and putting on a fake thankful face.

But in the intervening weeks, our first daughter was born, cutting short our Christmas shopping. On Christmas, I gave him a green plaid shirt, and he gave me—the antique egg. Now it became a treasure beyond belief. It was my *only* present, and symbolic of the birth of our daughter. That year we each received one gift, and we actually still remember what we got. That doesn't happen very often!

Over two thousand years ago, we received one unforgettable gift. However, we're not always thankful for the gift, and many don't even bother to accept it. We clutter up that gift with worthless trinkets and decorative knick-knacks. Some accept the gift but fail to unwrap all of the privileges that go with it.

No matter what you receive this Christmas, consider accepting the eternal present, wrapped in swaddling clothes and sacrificial love. And remember to thank the One who gave you this priceless gift.

Response: *Heavenly Father, May I never take the gift of Your Son for granted. I want to accept your precious gift anew. I believe in Your Son and want Him to live and reign in my heart. I know that He came, lived, died, and rose again for me that I might have eternal life. My heart is prepared to receive You as King, Lord Jesus. Come in, and may this Christmas be like no other Christmas before.*

December 23—All We Like Sheep

Light: "*I am the good shepherd; I know my sheep and my sheep know me—just as the Father knows me and I know the Father—and I lay down my life for the sheep*" (John 10:14–15).

Reflection:

With two-dozen sheep running around our backyard, I have new insight into sheep passages from the Bible. My descriptive vocabulary is limited, since we're not supposed to say "dumb" at Skye Moor Farm. So, for this devotional, I'll have to say our sheep are very "not-smart." I hate to admit it, but being compared with sheep is not exactly a compliment.

Sheep get lost easily; they are defenseless, non-aggressive, and submissive. Their worst predator is the domestic dog, which can chase them silly. If they fall over, they are sometimes unable, or unwilling, to get back up. You've heard of "cow-tipping," but probably not "sheep-tipping." When I find a ewe flipped over in the field, I have to right her myself. I am sometimes profoundly annoyed by the "not-smartness" of sheep.

Who took care of these "not smart" animals surrounding Bethlehem? Lowly, young shepherds with minimal education and spiritual knowledge.

Shepherds ate simple foods, endured harsh weather in primitive wild lodgings, and defended themselves against animals, lions, bears, wolves, and thieves, while protecting animals they didn't own.

Clothed in a heavy cloak, carrying the staff and rod, their familiar presence and voices were a reassurance to their flock. They cared for expectant ewes, newborn lambs, and sick animals needing special attention. They calmed the flock with a reed flute. At night, as the sheep entered the enclosure, the shepherd counted them with his rod and then slept at the entrance to protect them.[15]

The night Jesus was born, an angel revealed the good news to the least likely to receive a royal pronouncement. Shepherds must have a special place in God's heart! After all, God used plenty of shepherds throughout the Bible, and His Son Jesus called Himself the *Good Shepherd* (John 10). Indeed Christ's loving, protective, nurturing, and sacrificial qualities represent a good shepherd.

Who is your Shepherd? Whom do you follow and trust? An aria in *Handel's Messiah* quotes a passage from Isaiah 40:11 (KJV), "He shall feed his flock like a shepherd: he shall gather the lambs with his arm, and carry them in his bosom, and shall gently lead those that are with young." The soprano and alto each sing the tender lullaby. Don't you want to be fed by Him and carried by Him? Let the Good Shepherd of John 10 carry you through this Christmas season as you focus on the Good News.

Response: *Lord Jesus, thank you for being my Good Shepherd. Lead me in the right paths, guide me to still waters, restore my soul, and carry me when I am tired. In this Christmas season, may I never forget that You came to earth to show me the way. Help me follow You always.*

December 24—All Is Calm

Light: *While they were there, the time came for the baby to be born, and she gave birth to her firstborn, a son. She wrapped him in cloths and placed him in a manger, because there was no room for them in the inn* (Luke 2:6–7).

Reflection:

> *Silent Night, Holy night,*
> *All is calm, all is bright*
> *Round yon virgin mother and child*
> *Holy infant so tender and mild,*
> *Sleep in heavenly peace,*
> *Sleep in heavenly peace.*
> *Silent night, holy night,*
> *Shepherds quake at the sight*
> *Glories stream from heaven afar,*
> *Heavenly hosts sing Alleluia*
> *Christ the Savior is born!*
> *Christ, the Savior, is born!*
> *Silent night, holy night,*
> *Son of God, love's pure light*
> *Radiant beams from Thy holy face,*
> *With the dawn of redeeming grace*
> *Jesus, Lord, at Thy birth,*
> *Jesus, Lord, at Thy birth.*

Is all calm and bright at your home tonight? Maybe this lullaby is just what you need to focus on the manger, the heavenly hosts, the shepherds, and love's pure light.

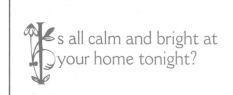

Is all calm and bright at your home tonight?

Though there are plenty of tales of zealous mice and a faulty organ, the beginnings of "Silent Night" are rooted in simplicity. In 1815, young Joseph Mohr became ordained as a priest and was assigned his first parish at Mariapfarr, a quaint village in the Austrian Alps. While at Mariapfarr, Mohr became accustomed to the down-home style of the local Christmas Eve Mass, where the musical repertoire included singing in the German language and accompaniment with folk instruments. This went against the tradition of the times that dictated that corporate worship could only be done in Latin. Father Mohr was so mesmerized by the Christmas worship of these country folk, it inspired him to write his own carol in 1816 he titled "Stille Nacht" or "Silent Night." A short time later, Mohr had been moved to the parish at Oberndorf, and there he incorporated the folk styles of worship he learned at Mariapfarr. His blending of German into the traditional Latin masses was popular among the parishioners, but met with stiff opposition among the episcopal hierarchy— especially fellow priest, Georg Heinrich Nöstler.

On Christmas Eve, 1818, Mohr asked Franz Gruber, schoolteacher, church organist, and choir director, to set the words to music with a guitar accompaniment. According to numerous accounts, the organ at the St. Nicholas church had broken down, forcing Father Nöstler to accept a midnight mass with an alternative musical arrangement. That evening in Oberndorf, Mohr and Gruber sang "Stille Nacht" accompanied by guitar. The choir echoed in four-part harmony, "Sleep in Heavenly Peace, Sleep in Heavenly Peace." This was the first time Mohr's carol was performed in public.

According to folklore, an organ repairman later found the lyrics to "Stille Nacht" in the St. Nicholas church. The repairman allegedly saved the words and melody for posterity and helped spread the word about the carol while on his travels. Once named "The Song from Heaven" it is probably one of the most powerful carols in evoking memories. Perhaps it does so most often in times when the world is not so still and silent.[16]

On December 24th 1914, the British and Germans were hunkered down in icy trenches on the Western Front. British troops saw twinkling lights near the German trenches. After looking into binoculars, they discovered the Germans were holding lighted Christmas trees above their heads. "Stille Nacht, Heilige Nacht" rang out and the British joined in, singing "Silent Night." Both sides laid aside their weapons and exchanged gifts, played soccer, and sang carols.[17]

Who wouldn't be calmed by the carol's simplicity? "Silent Night" is a beautifully gentle lullaby with a repeating rhythmic pattern reaching for the highest note on *heavenly* then falling to the lowest note on *peace*.

We want to feel that heavenly peace and the difference that one silent night can bring in our lives. We want *all is calm*. We want to see a gentle nativity scene, a snow-covered church, and peace on earth. And we want to know in our future *all is bright*.

This is the eve of something wonderful—the eve of celebrating the nearness and closeness of Immanuel. It may not be a silent night outside or a silent night in your life, but you can find a silent place in your heart as you reflect on this *Holy infant so tender and mild.*

Response: *My God and my Savior let me find a quiet place to worship You. Bless me with Your holy Presence and Your Spirit. I long to feel that all is calm because You are near. Let Your still, quiet gentleness overwhelm me. This is the moment before Your birth, the hush before Your Son is ushered into the world. Help me experience that anticipation anew.*

December 25—What Child is This?

Light: *"Today in the town of David a Savior has been born to you; he is Christ the Lord"* (Luke 2:11).

Reflection:

Who is Jesus, and why did He come? Are you surprised to find that question on Christmas Day? The song "What Child is This?" asks and then answers that question with "This! This! is Christ the King!"

William Dix, an insurance manager, is the lyricist behind this carol originally entitled "The Manger Throne." He was also a poet whose writing became more profound after a life-threatening illness left him bed-ridden for months. During this time, he studied the Bible and reflected on his own faith. He gave us this question-and-answer poem which was later paired with the Old English tune of "Greensleeves."

What Child Is This?

What child is this, who, laid to rest
On Mary's lap, is sleeping?
Whom angels greet with anthems sweet,
While shepherds watch are keeping?

This, this is Christ the King,
Whom shepherds guard and angels sing:
Haste, haste to bring him laud,
The Babe, the Son of Mary!

So bring Him incense, gold, and myrrh,
Come peasant king to own Him,
The King of kings, salvation brings,
Let loving hearts enthrone Him.

Raise, raise the song on high,
The Virgin sings her lullaby:
Joy, joy, for Christ is born,
The Babe, the Son of Mary!

The refrain for the last verse reveals His purpose on earth,

Nails, spear shall pierce him through the lamb of God for me for you.

What child is this? With this song and Luke 2:11, you have many names for the child whose name is above all names: Son of Mary, King of Kings, Christ, Savior, and Lord. Today, when many traditionally open presents, stop and read Luke 2:1–20 and give thanks for the present of His presence. May your *loving hearts enthrone Him* as you offer up thanksgiving and praise.

Response: *O Lord, You have given us the greatest gift. He is the Lamb of God, the King of Kings, our Savior, Christ the King, our Lord. Help me understand who You are so that I can celebrate Your presence and worship You with new intensity.*

December 26 —The Gift You've Always Wanted

Light: *Every good and perfect gift is from above, coming down from the Father of the heavenly lights, who does not change like shifting shadows* (James 1:17).

"Whoever has my commands and obeys them, he is the one who loves me. He who loves me will be loved by my Father, and I too will love him and show myself to him" (John 14:21).

Reflection:

Before Christmas one year, each adult in my family decided to draw names and give one special gift to the person on their slip of paper. The grownups heightened the suspense by keeping it all a secret until the presents were opened. On Christmas Day, the gifts were pulled from beneath the tree, and one by one they were unwrapped. At last we all shared the surprise of finding out the identity of each secret giver.

My quiet Dutch grandpa sat quietly with a present on his lap addressed *To: Grandpa.* At last he opened it and said proudly, "Just what I always wanted!" Everyone exchanged glances as he chuckled softly, but no one claimed to give this perfect gift. At last Grandpa shyly admitted, "I drew my own name."

When you opened your presents this Christmas, was there a gift that stood out among the rest because someone knew just what you wanted or needed? How *did* that person know what would please you? What *did* it take for him or her to give you the perfect gift? Did he or she spend time with you, observing you and asking questions?

Did you know God knows your name? He knows every thing about you (see Jeremiah 1:5). He knows exactly what you need and wants to give it to you. He is the giver of all perfect gifts.

But what if you wanted to give God a gift? How would you know what He wanted? The same way you choose a friend's gift. You need to spend time with Him and study about Him. You need to ask Him questions to know how to please Him and walk in His light.

> *Before I formed you in the womb I knew you, before you were born I set you apart; I appointed you as a prophet to the nations.*
> (Jeremiah 1:5)

Simeon received exactly what He wanted—seeing His Savior's face. Simeon gave God exactly what God wanted—a heart focused on Him.

This Christmas season, let's give back to God. Let's give Him the gift of seeking His face, focusing our hearts, and finding His purposes for our lives as we head into a new year.

Response: *Dear Father, I praise You for your many gifts to me. Thank you for knowing my name and my needs. May I seek Your face daily so I live a life pleasing to You. Help me know You better, and obey You fully, so I can give you gifts from my heart.*

December 27—God Meets Anna

Light: *For in this hope we were saved. But hope that is seen is no hope at all. Who hopes for what he already has? But if we hope for what we do not yet have, we wait for it patiently* (Romans 8:24–25).

Reflection:

When our first daughter Christine was born four days before Christmas, she became a gift that is still giving today.

From then on, no gifts could compare. Besides the gift of her *presence,* I loved her *presents:* a color-crayon portrait, a spontaneous hug, and a handmade ornament from preschool. In Parenting 101, no one explains the bewildering joy we feel from receiving the unconditional love of a child. No silk blouse, DVD, or perfume can compare with these serendipitous gifts of the season.

On that first Christmas, I wonder if Mary felt the same way. Surrounded by shepherds and animals, Mary had much to ponder. An expected baby took the spotlight in an unexpected and rude stable.

> Arriving in such an unexpected way, without beautiful packaging, God sent the Gift that keeps on giving.

Arriving in such an unexpected way, without beautiful packaging, God sent a baby to touch our hearts and to become the gift that keeps on giving.

The King of Kings found in a manger? Christ's followers didn't receive what they expected. Yet just as new parents delight in the unpredictable world of children, so, too, those seeking the Messiah became open to an unusual introduction. God was certainly creative in how he chose to meet us. I'm sure He's equally creative on a daily basis if we keep our eyes open for the unpredictable.

Anna had her eyes open. Anna had deep faith and hope that she would indeed see the Messiah. She lived for the realization of the promise. Anna expected to see the Messiah, and she was not disappointed. It didn't happen in her twenties, thirties, or even her sixties or seventies. God knew the right moment and the right place.

No angel visited Anna, no star stopped over her home, and she was not invited to the manger. Instead, Jesus met Anna in the place Anna called home: the temple

Anna experienced expectant living. We can learn from her. She and Simeon were looking forward.

When Christmas is over, we often think, *there's nothing to look forward to.* Sometimes there is disappointment. But, like Anna, we can look forward to deepening our relationship with God, as well as living with the ultimate hope of seeing Him face to face.

Response: *Dear Lord, teach me how to deepen my relationship with You. Help me look forward to meeting You face to face.*

Let me not look forward to and focus only on things of the world, but find fulfillment in seeing Your desires accomplished. Help me become like Anna, a woman of hope and expectation.

December 28—Journey of Faith

Light: *Come, let us bow down in worship, let us kneel before the* LORD *our Maker; for he is our God and we are the people of his pasture, the flock under his care* (Psalm 95:6–7a).

Reflection:

How far have you traveled this year on your journey of faith? Have you traveled through difficult times looking for consolation and seeking answers? Or do you sit asking questions but never seeking answers? If you looked at the cast of characters from the opening of the study, who would you be?

Consider King Herod. He asked where *the Christ* was to be found. He knew about a king, and yet unlike the Magi who traveled great distances, he wouldn't go five miles to find Him. He believed enough to fear, but he didn't believe enough to go and see. Neither did anyone else in Jerusalem.[18]

Are you like the shepherds? Have you heard exciting news and your new faith is so on fire, you run and share the Good News?

Or perhaps your journey of faith is more like Joseph's: one of trust and obedience, day by day leaving what is comfortable to do whatever the Lord commands.

Are you like Mary, whose faith was immediate and submissive, or are you like Elizabeth, who retreated to contemplate the miracle within? Elizabeth never entered the holy of holies, never spoke with an angel, and yet believed and recognized what was happening around her.

Or maybe you're like Zechariah, who couldn't quite get his mind around the most amazing encounter of his life. You're speechless, not because of wonder, but because of discipline by God.

Perhaps like Simeon and Anna, you show your faith by waiting and believing without having seen. You know God is working in your life and that Jesus is your hope.

> Perhaps like Simeon and Anna, you show your faith by waiting and believing without having seen.

The cast of characters is intriguing. They represent great variety in their lives and faith walks. Today, be the Magi. You've heard all about the Christ child, and you are on a journey moving closer and closer to your Savior. When you meet Him, believe and accept Him as your Lord. Bow down before Him in worship, and praise the name above all names.

Response: *Lord God, today I come to you on my knees. I bow down and worship You for who You are. You are my Lord, King, Creator, the Christ, and my Savior. I have come far in my relationship, and I will continue to follow You. Keep me on my knees daily, recognizing Your lordship in my life.*

Today, be the Magi. You've heard all about the Christ child, and you are on a journey moving closer and closer to your Savior.

December 29—The Gifts We Bring

Light: *"Do not store up for yourselves treasures on earth, where moth and rust destroy, and where thieves break in and steal. But store up for yourselves treasures in heaven, where moth and rust do not destroy, and where thieves do not break in and steal. For where your treasure is, there your heart will be also"* (Matthew 6:19–21).

But our citizenship is in heaven. And we eagerly await a Savior from there, the Lord Jesus Christ (Philippians 3:20).

Reflection:

Soon, you will remove this year's calendar from the wall, and with it, the accounting of your time. You will also gather your receipts, checks, and bills to enter the figures for your tax records, logging how you spent your resources.

There is another calendar of record—an awareness between you and God of how you spent your time, energy, and resources in your relationship with Him.

The Magi gave in many ways. They traveled far, brought expensive gifts, and fell on their knees in worship. Like the Magi, we can worship our Lord and offer Him all that we have. To do this we need to spend time in prayer discerning how to use the resources of time, travel, and energy. Then we need to give God the best. After all, He gave us His very best. The gift of worship is a great way to begin.

"Angels from the Realms of Glory" calls us to do just that.

The song's invitation repeats itself three times, each time on a higher note,

> *Come and worship, come and worship,*
> *Worship Christ the newborn king*

The words of this carol were written by Irishman James Montgomery and published as a poem entitled "Nativity" in the *Sheffield Iris* on Christmas Eve 1816. Montgomery usually published abolitionist pieces speaking out for Ireland's freedom; however, this carol was revolutionary in that it sought to unite instead of incite.

Ironically, many years later, a blind English composer named Henry Smart married his music to Montgomery's poem. His goal, like so many other carol writers, was to make the music of the English church more joyful. These two revolutionaries from opposing countries put together one truly inspirational carol of praise.

"Angels from the Realms of Glory"

Angels from the realms of glory,
Wing your flight o'er all the earth
Ye who sang creations story,
Now proclaim Messiah's birth
CHORUS
Come and worship, come and worship,
Worship Christ the newborn king.
Shepherds in the field abiding,
Watching o'er your flocks by night
God with man is now residing,
Yonder shines the infant light.
(REPEAT CHORUS)
Sages leave your contemplations,
Brighter visions beam afar.
Seek the great desire of nations,
Ye have seen his natal star.
(REPEAT CHORUS)
Saints before the altar bending,
Watching long in hope and fear
Suddenly the Lord descending,
In his temple shall appear.
(REPEAT CHORUS)

Each of the first three verses describes one aspect of the Nativity: angels, shepherds, and Magi. The last verse, like so many carols, reminds us to watch in hope and fear for the return of the Lord.

Response: *Lord, I am at the altar on bended knee. I am watching for You in hope and fear. I know one day You will indeed return. Teach me to long for Your reappearance. Prepare me for that glorious day.*

December 30—O Come Let Us Adore Him All Year Long

Light: *"You are worthy, our Lord and God, to receive glory and honor and power, for you created all things, and by your will they were created and have their being"* (Revelations 4:11).

Reflection:

One witty parent illustrated my holiday concert program by drawing notes on a musical staff. Those who could read music deciphered the tune and understood the double meaning in its title. "O Come All Ye Faithful" was the familiar carol—a tongue-in-cheek reference to the faithful parents coming out on a wintry night to sit for two hours on hard wooden bleachers.

"O Come All Ye Faithful" was originally written in Latin and entitled "Adeste Fideles." When the Roman Catholic Church and the Church of England were in deep conflict, John Francis Wade, an English Catholic, plainchant scribe and teacher, escaped to France where he preserved Catholic historical church music and later wrote this carol in the mid 1700s.

"O Come All Ye Faithful" has no rhyming pattern, but the melody line is easy to sing. Maybe that's why this carol has been listed at the top ten of the record charts three times. The verse and chorus are a dramatic contrast in melody. The verse sounds majestic and grand emphasizing a great call to come joyfully and triumphantly. Each line begs for an exclamation point at its end.

O come all ye faithful, joyful and triumphant,
O come ye, oh come ye to Bethlehem
Come and behold him, born the king of angels

But the chorus, with its repeating pattern ascending each time, moves us closer to the nativity, as though we've all tiptoed up to the manger and at last seen the Christ child.

O come let us adore him,
O come let us adore him
O come let us adore Him, Christ the lord

The next verse returns to glorious exclamations with the sopranos in descant scaling the heavens like a choir of angels.

Sing, choirs of angels, sing with exultations,
Sing all ye citizens of heav'n above
Glory to God, in the highest
All glory in the highest

The final verse recalls John 1:1–4, reminding us that *in the beginning was the Word* and Jesus is the *Word of the Father* made flesh.

Yea, Lord we greet thee, born this happy morning,
Jesus, to thee be all glory giv'n
Word of the Father, now in flesh appearing

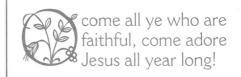

O come all ye who are faithful, come adore Jesus all year long. And in His presence may you feel His life and His light.

Response: *Dear Father, I adore You. I adore Your creation, Your love for me, and the gift of Your Son. Help me tiptoe to the manger and feel Your presence long after Christmas is over. May my adoration be pleasing to You, and may I dwell in Your light and life.*

December 31—Reordering Our Priorities

Light: *Teach us to number our days aright, that we may gain a heart of wisdom* (Psalm 90:12).

Reflection:

Less is more. More is not better. This isn't from the Bible, but it helps me. So often I add too many things to my list of activities. The problem is when each event arrives, I'm truly too tired to enjoy it. I've found that *less* enhances the activities I choose to do. Learning the art of saying, "no," helps make all the "yeses" more pleasurable.

A friend of mine writes a list of who she is and posts it near the phone. When the phone rings and she's asked to volunteer, she looks at her list:

Child of God
Wife of Frank
Mother of Mac and Paige
Sunday School Worker
School volunteer

Below her list she writes, "Just say no." When she declines another activity, she doesn't regret what she's missing, instead she considers what she'd miss if she *did* the added activity: quality one-on-one time, family nights, and peaceful evenings.

Put your priorities in order according to what you know the Bible is telling you, and then say "yes" or "no" accordingly. Remember, NOT putting priorities in order means every activity is equal. In other words, saying "yes" to too much lowers the status of all the "yeses" and demotes the people you care about most.

Let your goals reflect your priorities: God, husband, children, family, others. These priorities might result in the following goals:

1. Praise God in the morning.
2. Love my husband in his love language.
3. Speak gentle and kind words to my children.
4. Memorize a verse so I'm ready with good words (Proverbs 22:17–19).

Just like the psalmist, ask God how you can best spend your time to gain a heart of wisdom.

Response: *Dear God, teach me how to number my days. Help me not to waste time on the trivial but instead invest in the eternal. If I need to reorder my priorities, or change my activities, please reveal this to me through Your word and in prayer.*

January 1—The Turn of a Page. . . .

Light: *Therefore, if anyone is in Christ, he is a new creation; the old has gone, the new has come!* (2 Corinthians 5:17).

Reflection:

Happy New Year! Does everything feel new? Or does January 1st really feel any different from December 31st? Has anything really changed? The weather and our schedule certainly haven't.

Maybe the calendar should actually begin in September when everything changes. And yet, because the numerical year changes, we force ourselves to change, adopting resolutions to:

Lose weight
Exercise more
Spend more time with family
Get out of debt
Work less
Quit smoking or drinking
Do community service
Read more
Get organized
Live life to the fullest

But what if, on January 1, we only focused on *January 1st* by asking God, "Who do you want me to be *today*?" Yearlong commitments are worthy goals, but sometimes when we mess up, we're like the dieter who cheats with a Hershey kiss and thus downs three banana splits and quits working on her resolution.

If you're determined to make resolutions, make just two or three. Or instead of a resolution, commit to one verse you could live by for next 365 days and let the Word change you from the inside out.

> If you're determined to make resolutions, make just two or three.

Pick a verse or two from the Bible. Here are a few great ones to get you started: Philippians 4:8; Colossians 2:6–7; 3:1–4, 12–15. Make the verse(s) yours for the new year.

Try printing the passage on note cards. Tape one to your bathroom mirror and carry another in your purse so you're reminded of His Word wherever you are. Then believe January 1st and each day that follows will be different as you commit to living for Jesus through His Word.

Response: *Lord God, give me a scripture to live by this year and help me follow it each day. In addition to hiding it in my heart, may I live it from the inside out. May that life verse be evident to all who see me as I become newer each day in Christ.*

January 2 —The Greatest of These is Love

Light: *Dear Friends, since God so loved us, we also ought to love one another. No one has ever seen God; but if we love one another, God lives in us and his love is made complete in us* (1 John 4:11–12).

Reflection:

A Christian friend in college posted a sign above his door. It read FOR ME TO LIVE IS_____. Everyday when he left his room, he had to fill in the blank.

How would you daily fill in that blank? Who are you living for this year? Philippians 1:21 reads, "For to me, to live is <u>Christ</u>."

To *live in Christ* means to obey His commands by *loving in Christ*. In the Old Testament the reminder to *Love the Lord with all your heart and soul* was written on doorposts (Deuteronomy 6:4–9). Christ repeated this instruction, calling it the first and greatest commandment. Maybe all the resolutions in the world could be boiled down to: Love God. Maybe all those difficult choices and decisions we make could be filtered through the question, "Does it show I love God?"

Loving God necessitates loving others. Jesus said He wants us to love Him and love others so His joy will be in us and our joy will be complete (John 15:9–11). That's an amazing invitation and promise.

> *"As the Father has loved me, so have I loved you. Now remain in my love. If you obey my commands, you will remain in my love, just as I have obeyed my Father's commands and remain in his love. I have told you this so that my joy may be in you and that your joy may be complete.* (John 15:9–11)

As you enter and exit your home, consider filling in the blank, "For me to live is_____." Living and loving for Christ is a great way to begin the new year.

Response: *Heavenly Father, You love me in ways I can hardly fathom. Your amazing love sent Jesus to the cross for me. Help me remain in your love and obey your command to love others. Help me live for Christ, each day remembering this means to love You and others through Your strength.*

January 3—Joy to the World!

Light: *Let the rivers clap their hands, let the mountains sing together for joy; let them sing before the LORD, for he comes to* *judge the earth. He will judge the world in righteousness and the peoples with equity* (Psalm 98:8–9).

Reflection:

"Joy to the World!" Are you surprised we're still singing a carol? Actually, it's not really a Christmas song.

"Joy to the World" was originally titled "The Messiah's Coming and Kingdom." (Doesn't have quite the same joyful ring, does it?) The carol paraphrases Psalm 98:4–9, calling for all of creation to joyfully praise the reign of the Lord.

Isaac Watts, the man who brought us this joy-filled song, was frustrated by the dreary archaic hymns of his day. His father challenged him to come up with a hymn that expressed joy. He succeeded and ended up writing a new hymn each Sunday for 266 weeks for a total of 600 hymns in his lifetime!

"Joy to the World" is delightfully "singable" because it moves stepwise up and down the scale. Any child can approach the piano, start on a high "C" and play a downward scale for the opening of the carol. Many of the succeeding phrases also have upward and downward stepwise motion.

But ironically, there is little in this carol about Christmas. The first verse is often used in the context of His first coming, but the majority of the song declares Jesus' *second* coming.

Although "Let every heart prepare Him room," should have happened at His birth, we, too, are guilty of not preparing room in our heart for His *second* coming. On a day-to-day basis, we need to prepare our hearts to have room for Jesus and to be prepared to sing His praises. Nature declares His glory, and so should we!

Joy to the world, the Lord is come!
Let earth receive her King;
Let every heart prepare Him room,
And heaven and nature sing.

Joy to the world, the Savior reigns!
Let men their songs employ;
While fields and floods, rocks, hills and plains
Repeat the sounding joy

No more let sins and sorrows grow,
Nor thorns infest the ground;
He comes to make His blessings flow
Far as the curse is found,

He rules the world with truth and grace,
And makes the nations prove
The glories of His righteousness,
And wonders of His love

His kingship means He will reign in glory, truth, and righteousness. Satan will be bound, and Christ's kingdom will have no end! This is a song to sing year round. So stretch the Christmas season throughout the year and prepare your hearts each day by singing, "Joy to the World!"

Response: *My Savior, I'm thankful Your kingdom will never end! I loved your first coming and I long for Your return. All creation declares Your glory. When all heaven and nature sings, I shall join in! My heart prepares You room!*

January 4—Peace: The Gift of Reconciliation

Light: *"Blessed are the peacemakers, for they will be called sons of God"* (Matthew 5:9).

Reflection:

I enjoy watching Christmas specials with happy endings. I love a story where estranged family members are miraculously reconciled. For two hours I watch both sides of the arguments, and see how the characters build walls of anger and bitterness. And as the omniscient TV observer, I look for cracks of vulnerability where love, forgiveness, and healing can trickle through.

Although I don't enjoy hearing my dueling daughters argue, "But she did it to me first!" and don't like being the referee to their ranting, I know when I encourage apologies and forgiveness, they can begin anew and return to play.

It's tough for any of us to be the first to say, "I'm sorry." When my husband and I were first married and argued, I would say, "I forgive you" before either of us asked for it. At least it brought a reluctant laugh and maybe a quicker peace.

We can be peacemakers by forgiving and by accepting forgiveness. In this new year, keep your accounts short. Give yourself the gift of forgiveness, and you will be a healthier person emotionally, spiritually, and possibly even physically. Say, "I'm sorry," even if you think you're only a small part of the problem and

> In this new year, keep your accounts short. Give yourself the gift of forgiveness, and you will benefit emotionally and spiritually.

the other person started it. Forgive others immediately so you can get on with your life. Walls will crack. The saddest and most bitter people I know are those poisoned by hatred and the inability to forgive.

Then go one step further. Is there someone in your life with whom you are estranged? Let this be the year of healing. Step out in humility and ask forgiveness even if they "wronged you bigger." And if you're holding out, unwilling to forgive, forgive immediately so your Father in heaven will also forgive you (see Matthew 6:15).

Give yourself the gift of peace by being the peacemaker God called you to be. You will indeed be blessed as a son of God. That's a promise from the Prince of Peace.

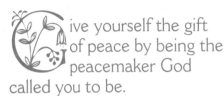

Response: *Prince of Peace, Help me to say, "I'm sorry," when necessary, and "I forgive you," with frequency. Bring to mind others I have hurt, and help me bring restoration and healing to those relationships. This year may I never let the sun go down on my anger, but seek resolution each day. Help me be a peacemaker and your child.*

January 5—A Christmas Lesson for the New Year

Light: *Therefore encourage one another and build each other up* (1 Thessalonians 5:11a).

Do not let any unwholesome talk come out of your mouths, but only what is helpful for building others up according to their needs, that it may benefit those who listen (Ephesians 4:29).

Reflection:

A white Christmas is rare in western Washington. That's what made Christmas 1989 all the more special. I flew home from the University of Michigan to a Seattle winter wonderland. The snow continued on Christmas Eve as my brothers, their friends, and I began creating the biggest snowmen we had ever built. We twenty-somethings were kids again rolling enormous balls of snow and hefting them taller than our height. Our creations were so full of personality wearing jewelry, scarves, and hats, we dubbed them Winston and Maggie. Winston with his moustache, and Maggie with her earrings and apron, posed proudly, delighting passersby. All day, drivers slowed to see the statues—many returning with cameras.

That evening as we played Monopoly by the fire, we heard suspicious noises outside. Much to our dismay, people had run through the yard and vandalized our sculptures. Our holiday spirit disappeared as we piled in a friend's truck to track them down. Thankfully, we never found the culprits, sparing them a tongue lashing for their disrespect.

There was something so discouraging in their destructive act. How could they be so cruel? Couldn't they appreciate the beauty of our creation?

That night, as I slept, I was awakened by voices in the front yard. I listened carefully. "They were so neat. I can't believe someone would do that. Let's try to build them back up!" And for the next few minutes, the new visitors attempted to restack, reshape, and recreate our originals.

In the warmth of my childhood bedroom, and in the depth of my heart, a piece of Christmas—and yes the "peace" of Christmas returned. Although one peek on Christmas morning told me Winston and Maggie could never be fully restored, I was touched that strangers cared enough to rebuild our snowmen. I was encouraged to realize our creations were considered of worth to others.

I learned a very important lesson that day: It is much easier to tear down than build up. And once something is torn down, the damage is not always repairable.

This year, can we value God's creation by challenging ourselves to build up the body and uplift others? God must love it when He hears us encouraging one another.

I had a health teacher in junior high who was a Christian. Across his desk was written: THREE. When I asked him about the number, he explained it was to remind him to compliment *three* kids per day. No doubt he applied the scriptures of encouragement and understood how valuable they were to the emotional growth of his students.

Isn't it awesome that we have such a powerful positive tool to use for God's glory? Let us step out in encouragement and love.

Response: *God of compassion, You encourage me in Your Word, help me encourage others with my words. Help me uplift others and let me see the delight in their reactions. May encouraging others become as natural as one-two-three.*

> Isn't it awsome that we have such a positive tool to use for God's glory? This tool is the gift of encouragement. Let us step out in encouragement and love.

January 6—Keeping Christmas All Year Long

Light: *Being confident of this, that he who began a good work in you will carry it on to completion until the day of Christ Jesus* (Philippians 1:6).

Reflection:

The best part of Christmas 1999 was actually *after* Christmas when my toddlers taught me that Christmas goes on and on and on. As three-year-old Christine rode through the grocery store in my shopping cart, she suddenly belted out, "BE NEAR ME LORD JESUS, I ASK THEE TO PRAY!" "Away in a Manger" couldn't have sounded sweeter.

Christine not only loved the music, she also loved the decorated Christmas tree. She turned the sometimes-depressing task of taking down the tree into a delight; and enjoyed the privilege of "legally" removing the ornaments, cherishing each one and the story it told. "Oooooooooo this one is sooooooooo cute, it makes me want to cry!" And when she accidentally broke one, she did cry. But it was an opportunity to tell her how much I loved her no matter what she did.

After the tree was bare, it stood for a day or two in our living room. One-year-old Julia was distressed by the missing angel, and Christine said, "I like it better with the lights and ornaments." When the tree was dragged to the far lower pasture, the girls felt sad. Christine kept talking about the tree, and I feared she would never get over the loss.

One morning she called out, "There's the Christmas tree!" *Oh dear*, I thought, *now she's imagining things.* However, she was right. The tree had blown onto our front walk by a ferocious windstorm. As we investigated the new arrival, Christine whispered, "It's sleeping."

Christine continued to play with her "untibbity" (nativity) set. She made characters talk, and carried the angel everywhere she went. Unfortunately, both girls liked to fight over Baby Jesus, which seemed to go against everything in the Christmas tradition.

One day when Christine asked almost hopefully, "Is Jesus on the cross now?" it showed me how much we want to celebrate life and His life, specifically. Her question helped me realize the celebration of love, joy, and peace, the surprises, and that the emphasis on finding Jesus in everything must linger beyond Christmas. Since God lives in us and loves us, our acts of love can continue throughout the year, all the way to preparing our hearts for next Christmas!

Why not try some of these ideas to help stretch Christmas into the new year.

Undecorating Party

Are you ready for another party? One of our favorite traditions is the "undecorating party." Set a day aside to celebrate taking down the decorations. January 6th (Epiphany) might be a great day.

Your party fare could include:

Christmas cookies

Gingerbread Trifle—Break the walls of your holiday house into tall glass bowls and pour pudding and whipped cream on top. Allow to set.

Angel Food Cake with crushed candy canes mixed in whipped cream

Peppermint Ice Cream Pie—crush chocolate sandwich cookies, top with peppermint ice cream, fudge sauce, and whipped cream.

White cake with peppermint candy thrown in the batter.

The Christmas Tree

Play your favorite carols one more time, and enjoy packing up the boxes of ornaments. The children love to help find the ornaments and gently wrap each of them—especially if they are their own. You could also begin an Epiphany tradition of searching for one last present hidden in the tree. If you are a post-holiday shopper, pick up a few marked-down ornaments to give your children to tuck away for next year.

As you "un decorate," plan secret mail. Write notes to yourself and to your kids and tuck them away in the boxes, so that next year there will be surprises in the decorations. Ask your kids to write notes to themselves about what they think they'll be like next Christmas, or how much they will have grown in height, or in Christ. Make a Christmas book to collect these.

If your kids can't quite part with the tree, it can be redecorated outside with edible ornaments (literally *for the birds*)!

Christmas Cards

Put Christmas cards in a basket and pull one out each day to pray for the sender. You can recycle the cards in several ways:

Create gift tags for the next year.

Make thematic collages for bedroom doors (e.g., Nativity, snow scenes)

Make new cards by cutting and pasting the old

Closing Ceremonies

Have a special post-holiday dinner and look at the past December's calendar. Debrief by starring the highlights. Keep your holiday highlights in your Christmas book. This will help you remember which traditions to continue. Together, write a letter to Jesus thanking Him for everything that happened in December and add it to your Christmas scrapbook.

Loving and giving should go on all year. Why not be a *Secret Angel* in deed in January instead of December? Consider someone who needs random acts of kindness, or have each child draw a family member's name and inundate that person with love.

Don't stop in January. After-Christmas traditions can continue into February. With a fourteen-day countdown to Valentine's Day, cut out fourteen different valentines for your wall and write one of the lines from 1 Corinthians 13:4–7 on each (e.g., Love is _____).

Make another links of love chain—this time seven red and seven white strips of paper with a loving action on each day to help count down to Valentine's Day.

Your heart can be prepared to make Christ the center of celebrations throughout the year.

Response: *Dear God, I have met with you for over two months. I loved being in Your presence, learning more about Your Son's birth, and why we celebrate the way we do. As I look toward spring, Easter, and new growth, may I continue to celebrate and grow in You. My heart is prepared, O Lord, to love you more each day.*

• • •

> Have a special post-holiday dinner and look at this past December's calendar. Debrief by starring the highlights. Together, write a letter to Jesus, thanking him for everything that happened in December and add this letter to your Christmas scrapbook.

Now for a little good bye from my heart,

"Thou Didst Leave Thy Throne" is an inspirational but relatively unknown carol. I love the words because they are in the first person using "me" and "my."

Thou didst leave Thy throne and Thy kingly crown
When Thou camest to earth for me,
But in Bethlehem's home there was found no room
For Thy holy nativity.
O come to my heart, Lord Jesus:
There is room in my heart for Thee!

What a theme song to remember our two months of study together. You have prepared your heart and prepared Him room. I hope through study, prayer, and devotionals, you have wonderful memories of this Christmas season. Throughout these months you've faithfully studied and prayed, now let me send you off with my prayer for you.

Heavenly Father,

My heart longs for these women to know You and love You so much that they can't wait to open the Word and look for Your direction. May they be inspired by being in Your loving presence and in fellowship with other Christian women who love them and encourage them.

Let them see You each day and celebrate Your presence. As they look at this year, may they see it filled with hope, for You are Hope; may they see it filled with opportunities to love, for You are Love; and may they experience great Peace, for You are the Prince of Peace.

They've studied your birth on earth, but You are born in hearts each day. May they understand that You are indeed Immanuel, God with us.

> I hope through study, prayer, and devotional readings, you have wonderful memories of this Christmas season.

Devotion Section Endnotes

1. Dr. Thomas Holmes, Dr. Richard Rahe, www.prcn.org/next/stress.html

2. Ace Collins, *Stories Behind the Great Traditions of Christmas* (Grand Rapids, MI: Zondervan, 2003), 184-88.

3. Ibid., 10–19; Paul L. Maier, *In the Fullness of Time: A Historian Looks at Christmas, Easter, and the Early Church* (Grand Rapids, MI: Kregel, 1991), 24–25, 29; Joseph J. Walsh, *Were They Wise Men or Kings? The Book of Christmas Questions* (Louisville, KY: Westminster John Knox Press, 2001), 69–70, 73–75.

4. Daniel B. Wallace, Th.M., Ph.D., *The Birth of Jesus Christ*, www.bible.org/page.asp?page_id=656.

5. Walsh, 46–47.

6. Maier, 24–25

7. Collins, 115–116.

8. Walsh, 25–26.

9. Ibid., 25–26; Collins, 115–116.

10. *Nelson's Illustrated Encyclopedia of the Bible*, ed. John Drane (Oxford, England: Lion Publishing, 1998), 158–159.

11. Beth Moore, *A Woman's Heart, God's Dwelling Place* (Nashville, TN: LifeWay Press, 1995), 210–211.

12. Walsh, 31–32.

13. Ann Stewart, *Happy Birthday, Jesus,* a Children's Christmas Pageant, 2001.

14. Collins, 178–83; Helen Haidle, *The Twelve Days of Christmas, The Story behind a Favorite Christmas Song* (Grand Rapids, MI: Zonderkidz, 2003).

15. Ralph Gower, *The New Manners and Customs of Bible Times* (Chicago, IL: Moody, 1987), 132–41.

16. http://www.silentnightmuseum.org/index.htm; Bill Egan, "SILENT NIGHT: The Song Heard 'Round The World," silentnight.web.za/history; "Joseph Mohr Gallery," Welcome.to/SilentNightMuseum.

17. Egan, "War and Remembrance: The Truce of 1914," Welcome.to/SilentNightMuseum; Walsh, 118–119.

18. Bob Deffinbaugh, Th.M, "Responses to the Revelation of the Coming of the King (Matthew 2:1–12, 16–18)," http://www.bible.org.

Christmas Carol Research—see sources used for Advent Bible study section

Appendix

Christmas Links of Love

Select 25 or more of the ideas listed below (either with your kids or surprise them with a completed strand). Write the ideas out on red and green strips of paper. As you link them together, alternate colors. (I find sometimes I need to look at my calendar as I put the links together. Some ideas fit better on weekends.) Consider making an extra set for friends!

Serve hot chocolate with a candy cane for stirring. Explain that the cane reminds us of the shepherds who first heard the news of baby Jesus. The white represents Jesus and purity; the red—His blood shed for us. Turn it upside down and it is a "*J*" for Jesus!

Cut out 25 stars and decorate them with glitter. Write the names of someone you know on each star. Hang the stars somewhere. Pray for that person on the day their star shines. You can even send your star to him/her and say you care!

Make your own wrapping paper from brown or white packaging paper. With paint or ink pads, use your thumb as a stamp and print multi-colored thumbprint lights. String them together with black lines to look like a string of old-fashioned Christmas lights.

Bake a "Happy Birthday, Jesus" cake with angel food cake, whipped cream, and peppermint candy shavings all over it!

Travel to Bethlehem tonight. Turn out all the lights except the tree. Pretend you're Mary and Joseph. Have a picnic with pita bread, fruit and nuts, olives, hummus, cucumber soup, yogurt, lamb, small round cheeses, and goat cheeses. Talk about what it was like to be Mary and Joseph. Read the Christmas story out of Luke 2.

Join the family together in a circle of light. Let each member light a candle and share an answered prayer and a request for the new year. Go around the circle.

Read Christmas stories at breakfast and after you tuck your kids in at night.

Attach a red or green bow and securely fasten a jingle bell to your pet's collar.

Create Christmas ornaments for your tree or packages by mixing 1 cup of applesauce, 1 and 1/2 cups ground cinnamon, and 1/4 cup of white glue. Chill dough for 30 minutes. Sprinkle cinnamon on waxed paper and roll out refrigerated dough 1/4 inch thick. Cut shapes with holiday cookie cutters. Poke holes in each ornament for hanging. Allow two days for drying. Enjoy the "cinnamony" aroma of Christmas.

Wonder as you wander beneath the stars tonight. How bright was the star of Bethlehem? Bring hot cocoa and a fuzzy blanket and gaze at all the stars God placed in the heavens.

Tonight at dinner, reminisce about memorable family Christmas activities and presents. Have each member fill in the blank: Remember when we _____? Remember when I unwrapped a _____?

Create a Christmas memory book for each year with drawings and thoughts for the month.

Enjoy a family night with popcorn, a fire in the fireplace, and everybody snuggled together to watch a Christmas movie.

Take a drive or walk to see all the holiday lights.

Place the magi far from your nativity. Let one child move them closer day by day.

Make cookies and write names of family members on them. Use them as edible place cards at dinnertime.

Outline your child's hands. Let them decorate and write TO: and FROM:. Cut out the hands for gift tags.

Make a fire in the fireplace and roast marshmallows. (For s'more fun, make sure you have chocolate and graham crackers.)

Plan a family sleepover beneath the Christmas tree. (For safety, turn out the lights before snoring!)

Fasten jingle bells on doorknobs for festive greetings and goodbyes.

Cover a door with gift wrap and make a tiny door nearby with the words "ELVES Only."

Record your family singing a merry Christmas carol on your answering machine.

Create an ornament unique to this current year. Hang it on your tree and plan to add a new ornament each year.

Pop corn, then string cranberries and popcorn to decorate your tree, door frame, or hearth.

Everybody write a special note to everybody else in the family. Tuck it beneath pillows before bedtime. Open the next morning.

Sing carols as loudly as you can. One person begins and stops and asks the next person to fill in the blank. "Jingle all the _____." "Let heaven and nature _____!"

Serve sleds for breakfast: French toast or pancakes with runners made of sausage.

Have breakfast for dinner one night.

Give everyone a certificate with someone's name on it. Ask each family member to write a *Gift of Service* for the person they have.

Call someone who doesn't receive many phone calls and sing merry songs of joy.

Take your artwork off the fridge and send it all to someone who doesn't have any "refrigerator art."

Start the day with a smile and try to make as many people smile as you can. Count how many smiles you gather in a day!

Try complimenting THREE people today. At dinner, talk about what you saw that you could compliment!

Start a jar of happy memories. Take an empty jar and say that in the year 20____ you'll fill it with ticket stubs, programs, and happy memories.

Have each child select a toy they don't play with much anymore and donate it to a local charity.

Purchase a new toy to donate to Toys for Tots.

Bake some cookies to give to a neighbor.

Invite a few neighbors over for dessert and coffee.

Play with the nativity set (if not breakable).

Take the whole family out to locate and cut down the perfect Christmas tree. Bring along a thermos of hot cider or cocoa.

Make shaped sugar cookies. Set out bowls of icing, sprinkles etc. Let kids decorate the cookies.

Roll a pine cone in peanut butter and sunflower seeds. Give the birds a holiday treat.

Bake cookies for your local fire department. Deliver them with a song.

Try out a new holiday flavor of ice cream.

Prayer Requests

Prayer Requests

Prayer Requests